THE CAMPUS SURVI

OR

How to Handle the Pot Situation

OR

How to Muscle in on the Big Thyme

OR

None of That Greasy Kid Stuff

OR

What to Do When the Heat's On

OR

How to Cut the Mustard

OR

How to Be a Flash in the Pan

OR

Get Off Your Rump and Put It in the Oven

OR

BOY! Can You Cook!

HOW to Select MEATS (page 18)

+ + + + + + + + + + + + + + + + +

THE CAMPUS SURVIVAL COOKBOOK

Got together by
Sean and Mike's mother
& Chris and Jon's mother

JACQUELINE WOOD &
JOELYN SCOTT GILCHRIST

Occasionally illustrated by
an Art Major who got locked in
overnight at the library

New York 1979

Stone Age Man courtesy of Carol Juliano

It is the policy of William Morrow and Company, Inc., and its imprints and affiliates, recognizing the importance of preserving what has been written, to print the books we publish on acid-free paper, and we exert our best efforts to that end.

Printed in the United States of America.

Wood, Jacqueline.
The campus survival cookbook.

1. Cookery. 2. Menus. I. Gilchrist, Joelyn Scott, joint author. II. Title.
TX715.W8824 641.5 72-100
ISBN 0-688-00030-4
ISBN 0-688-05030-1 (pbk)

12 13 14 15 16 17 18 19 20

To Stone Age men and women who must have poisoned themselves in droves tasting unknown plants; who warily learned to roast, broil, and stew some pretty strange cuts of meat; who heroically and brilliantly concocted the first beer and bread and soup; who invented SURVIVAL and most of the recipes in this book.

HOW to CUT UP Round OBJECTS (page 23)

+ +

CONTENTS

WHAT IT'S ALL ABOUT

IF YOU'VE FINALLY made it to your own apartment with a real kitchen in which you hope to eat cheaper, easier - but you don't know the first thing about cooking - how to shop for food, prepare it, cook it, clean up; if you don't even know what utensils to buy in the first place! - this book is for you. With affection. Cum laude. Trying to keep all those plates in the air - academics, athletics, music, love, peace, Freud, food - at the same time isn't all that easy.

Here you will find a solution to the feeding problem, anyway. Elementary recipes for solid, delicious meals, easy to prepare, and put together with an unblinking eye on the budget. There are dinner menus for 30 days which will average out at about $1.00 per meal, per person (early 1972 prices), plus shopping lists for each week. Also party recipes, Flat-Broke Specials, Exam-Week Specials you can eat all week, SURVIVAL! recipes (i.e., tasty health-kick recipes for minimum money).

Men, especially, should treasure the weekly shopping lists. The authors have often observed college students prowling grocery aisles, bewildered by the thousands of choices offered and filling carts with the most expensive trash foods in the store. If you take this book to the store, you'll cut shopping time <u>and</u> costs. (Note there is a section on how, where, and when to shop.)

We hope you will force yourself to follow, slavishly, the month's menus outlined here because they do have a pattern. Each Monday, for example, you get chicken. But each recipe explains a different, simple procedure that will be applicable to other things. The whole first week's recipes are a crash course in the basics of handling foods: fresh, canned, frozen, some of those repulsive-looking limp, raw meats. And then we go into spaghettis, eggplant (eggplant!), sour cream, etc. All recipes have been tested on college students and nobody threw up. They loved them, in fact, and were often amazed that delicious dishes contained ingredients they thought they loathed. So it goes. Give them a try.

Although the menus are balanced (offering protein, vitamins, minerals, carbohydrates), this is not a book on Hard Nutrition. Very few students can go whistling out the front door to return in a few minutes clutching edible roots, organic berries, and a sack of stone-ground flour. We hope you do read all about weeds and organic foods elsewhere and apply the knowledge to this book. However, all that is pretty useless if you don't know how to cook in the first place. This book, humanely, tells you how.

All daily meals are planned for <u>2 people</u>. Roommates. But which 2 roommates? Two college men? Two college women? One girl and one guy? Football players or bookworms? We thought it safest to plan the meals and set up the recipes to feed 2 normally hungry men. Women may find some of the main dishes over-generous and should cut back the quantities a bit or else learn to use up leftovers promptly.

If it's a question of feeding considerably more than two, later chapters have recipes that will feed 6 or 8. And, to multiply a recipe for 2, multiply every ingredient except the special seasonings (salt, spices, herbs) and add more of these last and to taste, if necessary.

All daily meals are planned for 2 people.

+ +

HOW to OUTFIT Your KITCHEN

WE HAVE TO ASSUME your kitchen is equipped with nothing but a stove and refrigerator because that's the way of most campus apartments - bare shelves, empty drawers, echoes.

You need utensils. How many? What kind? What for?

Here follows a list of bare essentials with which every daily menu in this book may be prepared completely to feed 2. If your cooking life gets more complicated than that, all our recipes specify what tools you need whether they're on the list below or not. Reasons for choice of particular materials - some the cheapest, some not - are given at the end of this section.

Even the bare essentials obviously demand an initial fast outlay of cash, at least $30 in the Year of the Price Freeze, Phase I, 1972. By now, things have no doubt changed. You can use our 1972 prices as a point of departure. THEY REPRESENT AN AVERAGE OF WHAT THINGS COULD BE BOUGHT FOR IN DISCOUNT HOUSES AND HARDWARE STORES. ONE SMALL HARDWARE STORE HAD FAR LOWER PRICES THAN EVEN THE DISCOUNT HOUSES. TRY COMPARISON SHOPPING.

Surely there must be some kindly relative who admires you, or is worried about you, or wants to take a tax deduction, who will make a gift of the more expensive items. Look plenty motivated and sincere when you ask for . . .

+ THINGS TO COOK IN +

One black iron skillet, 12" in diameter, for general cooking, about $5.

Plus an 8" iron skillet for eggs, frozen vegetables, etc., $2.50.

Get separate lids to fit these, about 50¢ a piece.

A 3-quart aluminum saucepan heats soups, boils spaghetti, costs $3.50. It should have a lid.

A Pyrex casserole - the 1 1/2-quart size costs $1 - must also have a lid.

See if you can find two aluminum cake pans, 8" x 8" or 9" x 9", for $1 each. You won't be knocking these around too much, so the cheapest is OK.

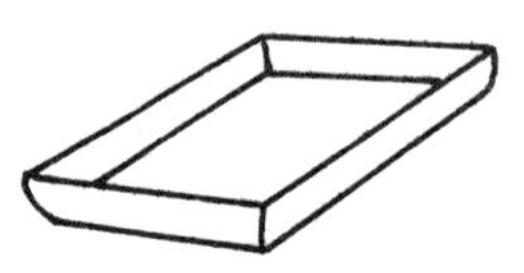

An open roasting pan, 13" x 9" x 2" cost $2.29 in rather thin aluminum; $3.79 in stainless steel. This will get hard wear, so get the heaviest you can afford - and one with a smooth bottom (not grooved), so you can make gravy right in the pan.

Get a cheap metal rack or two to just fit inside the roasting pan, so meats won't sit in their own grease while cooking; about 50¢ a piece. Use these same racks to cool cakes and bread.

That's all you need to cook in.

+ OTHER NECESSITIES +

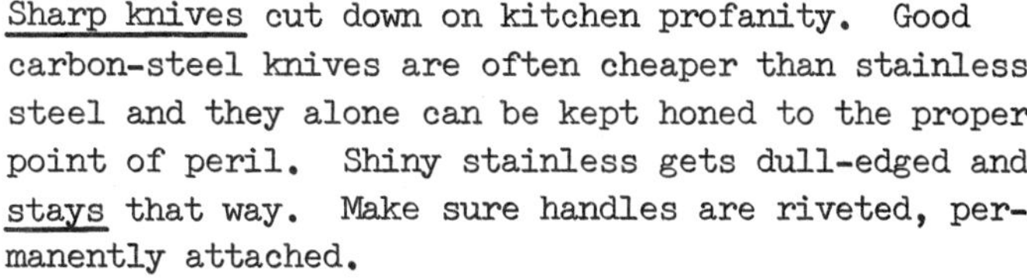

Sharp knives cut down on kitchen profanity. Good carbon-steel knives are often cheaper than stainless steel and they alone can be kept honed to the proper point of peril. Shiny stainless gets dull-edged and stays that way. Make sure handles are riveted, permanently attached.

For larger cutting jobs this knife seems to be a good shape. The best size is 6" blade and 4 1/2 handle: it'll cost about $6.

A carbon-steel paring knife with 3" blade should cost about $3.

Pick up a whetstone, preferably with a handle, about $1.50, to keep knives sharp. Ask the hardware man to show you how to use it properly. This is important. Remember that non-stainless knives will rust, so always wipe them perfectly dry.

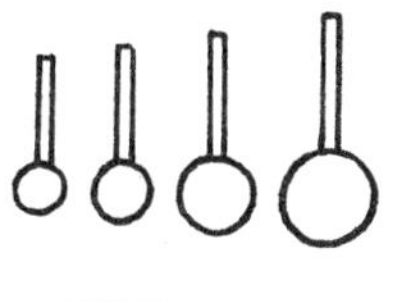

Metal measuring spoons don't break or melt (as plastic ones do) if left near heat; about $1.50.

A 16-ounce (2-cup) Pyrex measuring cup for 79¢ lets you measure easily by the see-through method.

Long-handled wooden spoons, 3 for 85¢, won't conduct heat, won't burn fingers. You can let them stand in the pot.

You'll be surprised how often you use a good strainer (sieve). For $1.29 you get one with handles and legs that drains spaghetti, dries lettuce, and sifts marijuana.

Also get a slotted spoon for 69¢ to serve vegetables without slopping liquid all over the plate.

Surely there must be some kindly relative

+ +

who will make a gift of the more expensive items?

+ +

A slotted spatula does the same thing for bacon and eggs, dropping the grease back into the skillet.

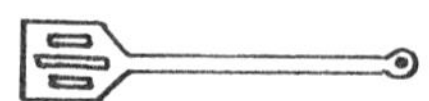

Sometimes you see a set of 3 or more slotted utensils for $1 and it may last out the year for you.

Pick up some kind of bottle/can opener combination and not electric - that's expensive, temperamental, and takes up counter space.

A small basting brush for 25¢ is useful for swabbing barbecue sauce on things.

A wire whisk is absolutely invaluable for smoothing lumps out of sauces and gravies.

A nest of 3 or 4 plastic mixing bowls, fairly sturdy, will cost about $1.50.

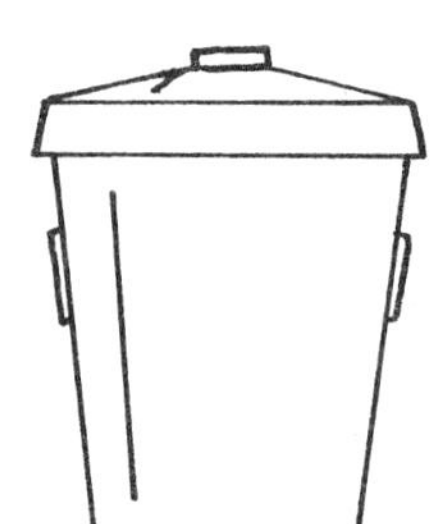

A college friend was puzzled by the poisonous sweet smell haunting his apartment. Trained sleuth-work led to his kitchen trash can with one of those Easy-Push-Open tops. No good.

Actually, you should empty trash can daily, but you probably won't. Always line the can with grocery sack, and use a 6-gallon heavy plastic can with a lid that clamps shut; about $2.79.

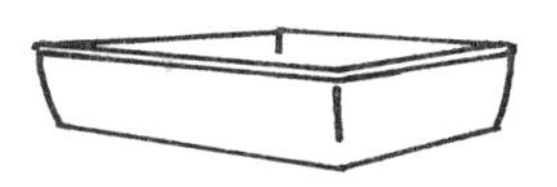

If you don't have a divided sink, get a small round or oblong plastic dish pan to soak utensils without making the single sink unusable. For easy clean-up, a long-handled sink brush with stiff bristles; about 69¢.

A dish drainer, at $2.69, stacks dishes to dry by themselves. But you'll still need about 6 cloth towels to dry knives, pans. You'll use paper towels, but ponder that they cost 49¢ to 79¢ a pair and that 2 cloth towels cost as little as 59¢. Throw them in with the weekly wash and you can use them all year.

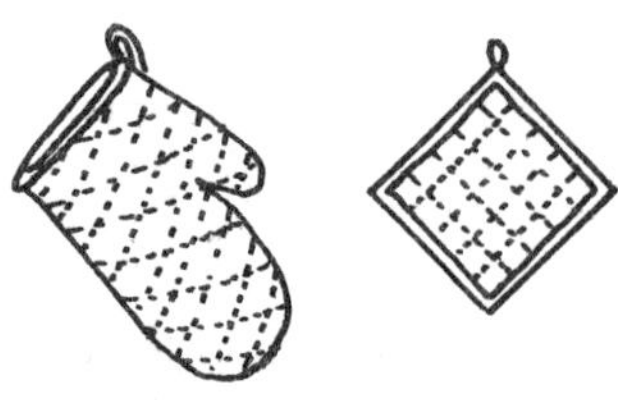

Pot holders are essential. Get 2 heavy ones.

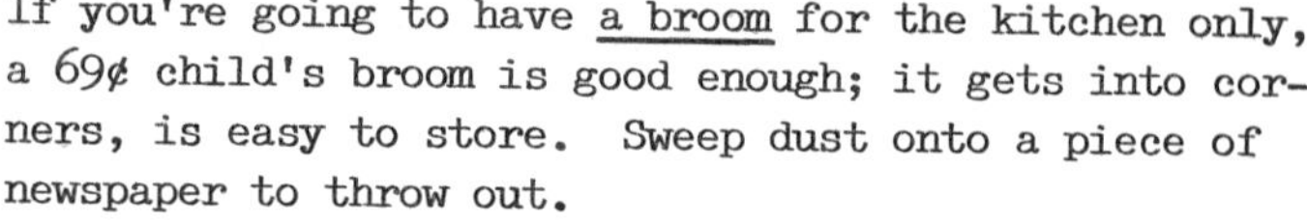

If you're going to have a broom for the kitchen only, a 69¢ child's broom is good enough; it gets into corners, is easy to store. Sweep dust onto a piece of newspaper to throw out.

You still need salt and pepper shakers, about 50¢ a pair.

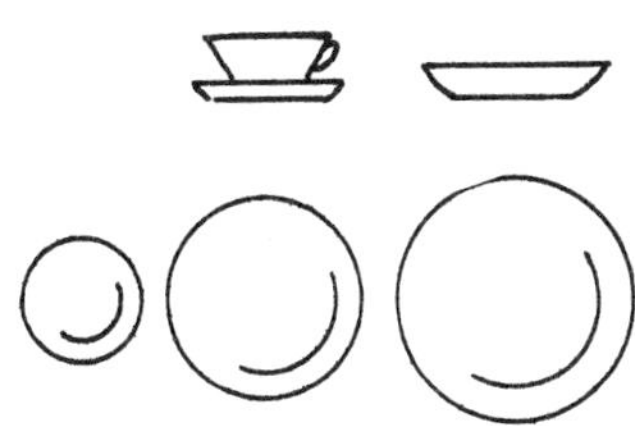

A set of dishes for four. Prices vary enormously but perhaps you can promote these, and eating utensils, from someone charitable. Really cheap stainless tableware is no bargain because the tines of the forks are rough, unpolished on the inside. These areas tend to collect food and germs and are hard to clean.

Keep track of what you pay for everything and you'll know what price to ask when you want to sell it all.

+ NON-ESSENTIAL ITEMS, BUT HANDY +

Toaster
Coffee pot
Rubber spatula
Long-handled kitchen fork
Extra saucepan
Pitcher for mixing frozen juices
Vegetable cutter
Bread loaf pans
Meat thermometer
Splatter lid
Kitchen scissors
Serrated stainless bread knife
Cookie sheet
Cheese grater
6 to 8-quart soup pot
Large party casseroles

+ WHY CHOOSE WHAT PAN? +

Cheap, thin-bottomed pans are maddening. Handles fall off. Dents appear which collect food, making them hard to clean. The really bad news is that thin pans develop "hot spots," places where the metal is permanently weakened and foods will proceed to burn in that same spot every single time. A burned flavor can ruin a whole dish - not to mention the difficulty in cleaning the pot! In buying pans remember that you may re-sell them some day. And so we suggest: BLACK IRONWARE SKILLETS. They're cheap, completely reliable, all professional kitchens are full of them. NOW HEAR THIS: The first few times you use each iron utensil, coat the entire inside with cooking oil BEFORE and AFTER using it. This will prevent rust - which is iron's other problem besides weight. All iron skillets today seem to have a sticker that says "Pre-Seasoned, Ready to Use." Don't believe it. Oil the skillets religiously until they acquire a satiny-smooth look. You should be able to sell used ironware for its original price. If kept oiled, it will be in better shape than when you bought it.

ALUMINUM and STAINLESS STEEL saucepans are fine. Get the heaviest you can afford and make sure handles are riveted on.

NON-STICK PANS: How nice if they held up, but we've never seen one, used daily, that did. No matter how courteously you treat it, the non-stick surface will wear away, or peel off, and the pan ends up with a marred surface which you don't know how to clean and which will stick.

COPPER PANS: Great, but too expensive. And we wonder just how many ancient people were poisoned by copper utensils before someone invented the tin linings! The lining on a copper pan must be replaced regularly or it's lethal.

ELECTRIC SKILLETS: A 12" size is available from $15. Heat is so well controlled that there's little chance of burning things. Drawbacks are that they're awkward to store, usually end up taking valuable counter space, and the cords are too short so you must have an electrical outlet very close by. Also, all inexpensive ones seem to have that non-stick coating that wears off.

PYREX: A form of heat-proof glass which is very good, and cheap. Most Pyrex can be used only in the oven, not on direct flame.

ENAMELWARE: Discolors and chips very quickly but a 6- or 8-quart soup kettle with lid is cheap, about $4, and is perfect if you intend to get a big pot of something going (see Parties and Exam-Week Specials).

+ BASIC KITCHEN STAPLES +

These staples will get you through all four weeks of daily menus. You can buy them all at one whack, or purchase just the staples for recipes you decide to cook. Or, if you follow our weekly-menu plan, you can shop from the lists of necessary staples that are given at the start of each week.

Bread
Butter or margarine
Coffee
Tea bags
Eggs
Milk
Fruit juice
Sugar
Brown sugar
Flour (unbleached or stone-ground, if possible)
Salt
Pepper
Salad oil (corn, peanut, or safflower), 24-oz. size
Vinegar (wine or cider), 1 pint
Prepared mustard
Dry mustard
Garlic powder
Lemon juice (bottled)
Vanilla extract
Paprika
Oregano
Thyme
Basil
Bay leaves (optional)
Curry powder
Instant minced onion
Bouillon cubes (chicken and beef)
Ketchup
Worcestershire sauce
Mayonnaise (Hellmann's)
Potatoes
Onions
Garlic bulb
Celery and carrots (for snacks)
Fruit (for snacks)

HOW to SHOP

1. Shop in the same store each time.
2. Never shop when you're hungry.
3. Shop only once or twice a week.
4. Be wary of sale items.
5. Think "percentages."

1. SHOP IN THE SAME STORE because it's easier to locate things, because you can make friends with a butcher who can be mighty helpful, and because you can soon estimate the times when it is least crowded. Shop at those times.

2. NEVER SHOP WHEN YOU'RE HUNGRY because it leads to impulse buying. Besides being expensive, you will clutter your few shelves with all those things (lump crabmeat, exotic sardines) which will always seem too costly or too mysterious to open. Buy only what's on the list or what you decided on in advance. The less time spent shopping, the less money spent.

3. SHOP ONLY ONCE OR TWICE A WEEK, preferably toward the weekend, because fruits and vegetables are fresher, and because most stores have weekend specials which are great money savers - especially the meats. Specials are listed in newspaper ads and are posted in stores. Once you have run through the month's menus given here, concentrate on cooking meats which are weekend specials, using recipes indexed.

4. BE WARY OF SALE ITEMS. If you get highly enthusiastic about a 20-pound turkey because it's only 29 cents a pound, remember that you may be eating it for weeks. "Eternity," some sage said, "is a 10-pound ham and two people." And then, what doth it profit a man if he gain a whole 25-pound sack of potatoes for only 63 cents, then suffer the loss of most of them because they mold or turn into smelly little shrubs before he useth them?

5. THINK PERCENTAGES. If one can of soup costs 9 cents, the next 10 cents, you're really not talking about "just a penny more." On the dollar, you're talking about a 10% increase! Notice that most chain stores have canned foods under their own labels. These are usually of good quality and cheaper than brandname products. Sometimes they're even made by the same firms as the brandname ones for sale under the chain-store label.

Look into quantity buying with friends; you can save money buying by the case, or bushel. BUT, communal buying needs a firm manager. If you can locate a canonized saint with a mathematical mind who owns a half-truck, he's your man.

Frozen TV dinners and packaged prepared foods are extremely EXPENSIVE in every way. You pay for the packaging, the advertising, the labor to make the stuff, plus all the chemical additives necessary to preserve it. Meals you prepare yourself will be tastier, cheaper, and far more nutritious.

+ +

HOW to Select MEATS

+ +

PERHAPS you've already discovered that you can't turn every nice big slab of red meat into a juicy sirloin by simply shoving it under the broiler. If mistreated, any meat can turn into linoleum. So, it's always a good idea to be pleasant with the butcher. Tell him what plans you have for the meat (broil, fry, stew, etc.) and he'll probably help you select the right cut.

+ +

For PURISTS who prefer a more clinical, anatomical approach to the subject, we wrote to our friend Greg (who's in pre-Med). We give you his letter in its entirety:

HOWDY
Cant seem to finf a table thats the right height for me yo work at this typewruter but her goes.

Beef cuts are easy to understand if you will pretend youre a steer waking around on all fours. A steer is a bull that's a enuch so it gets fat fatser.(wish you han'dt asked me to type this thing)

snimsld str judy likr proplr

Well well. Better move left hand over.

Animals are just like people. Tender cuts are from muscles seldom used. The Tenderloin, or Filet Mignon, is a muscle rught nexxx to the backbone and a steer would have to be a contortionist to use it much. The rib roasts, Sirloin and Porter_horse steaks are right there too. This anatomical position makes them all tender cuts and more xepensive. You can broil all these. As a matter ofact you can practically eat them raw, which is "very rare.

Take the tail. The steer swishes it around a good deal getting rid of flies. Thats tough (I mean the meat isO) but a tail is loaded with flavor because it has lots of cartilage. You cook it a long time and it makes fine soup. They always call it Ox-tail. I think it should be called just plain TAIL because it makes you wonder where they found an ox.

Now about this CHUCK that you use all through your cookbook. Where does it come form? the front shoulder area. If you were on all fors you wouldn't use it much, but a litle. So its medium tender. If you see a piece of chock that has lots of Fat rumming through the meat, all pink and pale instead of ruby red, you can do wonders with it because that fat disintegreates, basting the meat while it cooks. Some Chick can have a better flavor than a Sirloin.

ROUND STEAK is usually tougher than Chuck because it comes from the top of the back leg. Since the animla used the muscles more often (doing various things) it contains less inner fat. Round Steak has to be cooked in a liquid, or tinderized, to make it tender. hAMBURGER is just smashed odds and ends i'd rather not go into. (You wouldn't beleive what some butchers grind up!) Buy Ground Chuck.

I am really very sory about this typing.

OK. Pork: You"re still on your hands and knnes. Right? And you eata lot because you're a pig. Bacon comes from the fat stomac. The tender chops and Roasts are near the spine plus the Tenderlion (which is called Canadian Bacwn when it's smoked) A HAM is the top of the back leg which you might have guessed. The Boston BUTT is a fooler. It doesn't come from the butt at all but from the pig's front shoulder, which syas something about Boston. In other cities that general shoulder area maybe called a Cottage ham or Picnic. Ask the butcher whatswat.

Just remember to cook pork, <u>ALL</u> prok, a long time. This electric typewroter has got to go!

Lam. What the hell. Americans always xook the hell out of LAMB. Wyh? It should be served rare, or meduin rare, like beef. It's tender, young animle. Why incinerate ut?

I can't stand this

A picture is worth 1o,000 wrods. Here is a picture.

LOVE GERG

+ + + + + + + + + + + + + + + + + + + +

+ +

If you get down on all fours, you can tell which muscles are used the most.

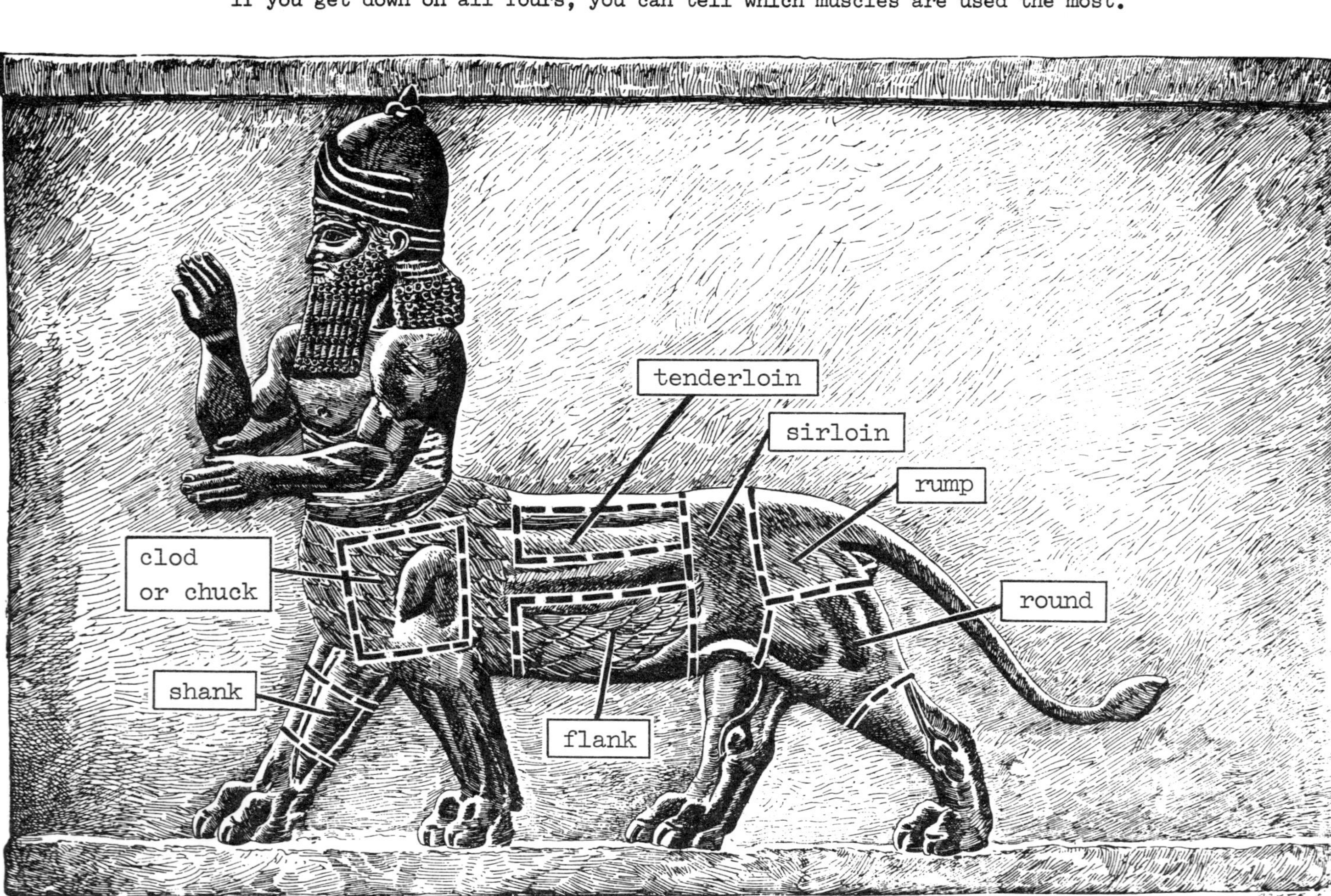

HOW to STAY OUT of the KITCHEN

YOU WILL never (never, never, NEVER) "feel like doing the dishes tomorrow." This is a great natural law, like water seeking its own level or $E = mc^2$.

Paper plates are out (pollution, etc.). Just digging into the pot with your right hand like an Arab isn't a bad idea, but it takes practice and probably isn't locally acceptable.

And so, before you cook anything, fill a small plastic dishpan (or the second sink, if there is one) with hot soapy water, and throw each thing into it to soak instantly after use. This cuts cleanup by about 90% and you won't have to face that nauseating collage of petrified grease and stuff in the morning.

Reliable private testing has proved that the world's hardest substance is not the diamond, but glued-on egg yolk. No doubt the Sphinx would have been carved of it if the Pharoahs had owned enough chickens and it would still have its nose today.

Dirty dishes piled around attract roaches and ants. There's no surer way to turn off that pretty girl who's making the salad for your soiree than to let her see a few of those armored beasts with twitching antenna scuttling here and there. Don't let down your guard. Remember that roaches are smarter than you are. They are lightning quick spawn in nightmare quantities, and are practically immune to poison unless it's given to each bug intravenously.

So. Try to be a nut on this neat and clean thing. Soak pots and utensils. Do dishes at once or let them soak in soapy water, they'll clean themselves. Arrange shelves with surgical neatness. Keep them that way. It'll help to keep you OUT of the kitchen.

HOW to COPE with LEFTOVERS

THE SOLUTION to this problem was one of primitive man's first triumphs of domestic genius. He turned the wolf into that amiable camp follower and disposal we call "dog." Why don't you get one? Back at Camelot, dogs were also used as handy roving napkins. We're not really suggesting this, of course, although the idea is picturesque.

The real answer is to throw leftovers OUT when no one is looking.

But waste bothers you? You're concerned about those skeletal millions starving in Bombay. Bravo! Pursue this! If you can figure out how to ship two tablespoons of peas and a small bowl of bacon grease over there, please let us know at once.

We decided long ago that no matter how may gelatinous mushy little mounds of this and that we ate, it wasn't going to fatten those people in India. Our recipes here are generally designed to produce no leftovers, except for the Saturday roasts. Just in case, however, there are suggestions for using leftovers scattered here and there.

AND - now this is important - it is possible to have a SYSTEM about leftovers. It may not take care of absolutely everything, but it is remarkable, nevertheless. It's called SURVIVAL BONE SOUP and is discussed at length on page 142.

+ +

HOW to FIGURE Kitchen MEASUREMENTS

+ +

t. = teaspoon
T. = tablespoon

c. = cup
pt. = pint
qt. = quart

oz. = ounce
lb. = pound

+ + + + + + + + + + + + + +

3 t. = 1 T.
2 T. = 1/8 c.
4 T. = 1/4 c.
8 T. = 1/2 c.
12 T. = 3/4 c.
16 T. = 1 c.
1/4 c. = 2 oz.
1/2 c. = 4 oz.
1 c. = 8 oz. = 1/2 pt.
2 c. = 16 oz. = 1 pt.
4 c. = 2 pt. = 1 qt.

1 lb. granultted sugar = 2 c.
1 lb. powdered sugar = 2 2/3 c.
1 lb. brown sugar = 2 2/3 c.
1 lb. sifted flour = 4 c.
1 lb. butter = 4 sticks
1/4 lb. butter = 1 stick
1 stick butter = 8 T.
1/2 stick butter = 4 T.
3/4" off a stick of butter = 2 T.
3/8" off a stick of butter = 1 T.
Thin slice off a stick of butter = 1 t.

+ + + + + + + + + + + + + +

Garlic: 1 medium clove = 1/8 t. garlic powder
Herbs: 1 T. fresh = 1 t. dried
Mushrooms: 1 lb. fresh = 6 to 8 oz. canned
1 lemon = about 3 T. juice

+ + + + + + + + + + + + + +

Honey versus sugar: In baking breads or making pie fillings, substitute 1 c. honey for 1 c. sugar.

In baking cookies, cakes, substitute 7/8 c. honey for 1 c. sugar, and reduce liquid called for in recipe by 3 T. for every 1 c. honey substituted.

HOW to TACKLE a STOVE

WE ASSUME the stove's pretty minimal. Four burners on top. A door underneath. A sort of drawer at the bottom. Some knobs. The oven knob has temperature settings. Those are for baking and roasting (see below). The knob also has a setting for "Broil" that controls the appropriate heating element.

On stove top: Boil, simmer, fry and saute, in saucepans and skillets.

In oven, if ELECTRIC stove: Bake and roast with bottom heating element, door closed.
Broil with top heating element, oven rack 7" away from heat, door ajar.

In oven, if GAS stove: Bake or roast, door closed.

In bottom unit ("drawer") if GAS stove: Broil, rack or broiling pan 5" away from heat, unit closed.

The empty bottom drawer of an electric stove is a good place to keep iron skillets.

For roasting: Accurate oven temperature is important. Generally your local gas and/or electric company repair man will check your oven's accuracy free of charge. (Telephone to find out first.) If not, get a reliable oven thermometer at the hardware store. If you can't get the oven setting and the thermometer reading to match, get the stove fixed. Find an engineering major, give him a beer. Maybe he'll know how to cope. Or resign yourself to mathematical calculations to compensate. (Write these down! Don't do them again.)

HOW to CUT UP Round OBJECTS

AT EVENTIDE, when skies deepen to purple and birds soar to their nests, etc., the serenity of twilight is rent with a grim sound - the amateur chopping of onions, a relentless hacking, scattering, stabbing, and retrieving of elusive slippery scraps.

HOW to CUT UP Round OBJECTS

Very few people know the trick of chopping a round object with racing speed. Therefore recipes which demand dicing or slicing of mushrooms, carrots, or ONIONS! seem too discouraging to try.

You would be smart to learn the professional trick of chopping. It takes a few weeks of off-and-on practice to get good at it. After this, you will save quantities of time, no recipe will daunt you, and you may even enjoy showing off your skill, nonchalantly.

If you can chop an onion, you can chop anything. The technique works for all round, firm objects. Start by slicing.

+ HOW TO SLICE AN ONION +

You need a fairly long, very sharp knife, a peeled onion, a cutting board.

1. Cut onion in half, from top to bottom, through the root.
2. Place one half on board, flat side down. Because of this cut side, you can hold the onion down firmly with left hand.
3. Now cut across the width of the onion many times. Do other half. It's sliced.

+ HOW TO CHOP AN ONION +

Ancient Egyptians considered the onion sacred - its many complete layers sinnified many lives. Because of these layers, an onion will fall apart into chopped pieces easily if cut correctly.

1. Cut a peeled onion in half through the root, as above.
2. Place one half on cutting board, flat side down, root pointing left.
3. With thumb and fingers of left hand, hold onion sides firmly. With right hand, point tip of knife to root. Make many thin slices the length of the onion, but do NOT cut quite through the root. The solid little root holds the onion together for the final operation.
4. Press onion together firmly with left hand. Now delicately but firmly make thin slices across the width. (If your knife isn't really sharp, you'll have to gently saw a little.) Do this slowly and perfectly. The onion will fall into small dice in a nice neat pile.

+ TO CHOP A GARLIC CLOVE +

Do this right over the pan without using a cutting board. You need a small, sharp knife, a peeled garlic clove.

1. Hold root end of clove in fingers of left hand.
2. Small knife in right hand, make a neat cross-hatch of about 10 deep cuts into the clove at the opposite end, but don't cut through the root.
3. Now, as if you were cutting a spliced wire, cut across the clove many times. It will fall into tiny dice right into your pan. Chip the root end into tiny pieces if you want. All done.

\+ + + + + + + + + + + + + +

+ +

FIRST THINGS FIRST

+ +

+ HOW TO KEEP YOUR GIRL FROM GETTING PREGNANT +

Say you are given a new racing Ferrari which you will be forced to drive for the next seventy-five years. No doubt you'd clean the motor with Q-Tips and hover over its gas and oil mixtures like a French chef pouring aspic.

In exactly the same way, you are imprisoned in the vehicle of your body (for seventy-five years!) with a chassis which can never be exchanged nor replaced. Poor fuel reduces your speed because it starves your body, mind, and spirit. Don't blame those psychological problems all on early home life and your parents. You may be creating your own problems right now - at least not actively correcting them - by constant consumption of Non-Foods, those over-processed,

Is she? Or isn't she . . . ?

+ + + + + + + + + + + + + + + +

over-priced products which litter our grocery shelves. Some actually contain a dozen or more chemical additives and who knows what they will do to us in the long run!

A weak diet of sweet breakfast cereals, potato chips, popcorn and pizza is exactly like syphoning Fresca into your Ferrari gas tank.

Acne, lack of confidence, that feeling of being tired all the time, inability to concentrate, irritability - these are all symptoms of a poor diet. You can correct them.

Breakfast is man's fuel injector. A high-protein breakfast of eggs or hamburger, milk, and toast lets energy into the body slowly over a long period of time. A sugary breakfast gets you going fast, like gunning a motor, but the energy is quickly gone. Each morning, Americans consume orange juice, cereal, toast, and coffee as if it were some hallowed religious ceremony. But professional athletes and hard-working country people the world over start the day with plenty of solid, energy-packed foods like beef stew, soup, cheese, sardines, slabs of good bread, olives. They seem to lead strong, productive lives, so why don't you cultivate a big breakfast habit?

After all, why always fill yourself with a big meal at night, then sleep off the energy? Eat some of that protein in the morning. Check out breakfast the night before. The mere thought of something delicious waiting may help to get you up.

Oh, yes.

How to keep your girl from getting pregnant?

The only really foolproof method, applicable to the Cro-Magnons right on through to Madison Avenue, is to stop screwing.

Right on! ladies. Of course you knew this all along.

However, we'll admit - now - that the subject is, as the saying goes, outside the province of this book. We wrote that headline in an attempt to make sure you would read these pages about breakfast. They're THE most important ones in the book, so we hope you'll forgive.

+ + + + + + + + + + + + + +

+ NO-TIME-FOR-BREAKFAST BREAKFASTS +

1. Eggnog: Open an egg or two into a cereal bowl. Add 1 heaping tablespoon sugar, 1/4 teaspoon vanilla extract. Beat this with a fork or wire whisk, using a circular motion, until light and frothy. Pour it into a tall glass, fill with cold milk. Stir. Drink. (You can make eggnog the night before. Refrigerate. Stir again. It will be ice-creamy.)

2. Bowl of vanilla ice cream. Emergency measure only. Refreshing for a hangover, though.

3. Pancakes and a glass of milk. Make batter the night before (from a pancake mix; instructions on box) and refrigerate. Lightly grease skillet, spoon thin batter in in small quantities so it will cook fast, brown in seconds. Eat with honey, syrup, or jam. (A spoonful of wheat germ in the batter is a good idea.)

4. Eat anything leftover that's palatable cold, such as roast chicken, ham, etc.

5. Drink a glass of milk and grab an apple to eat on the way.

6. Baked eggs: (You dress while these cook.) The minute you get up, turn oven to 350. Melt 1 tablespoon butter in small skillet on top of stove. Add 2 eggs, place in hot oven. By the time you're dressed, 8 to 10 minutes, eggs will be ready.

7. Cold hard-boiled eggs: Eat with a touch of salt and Worcestershire sauce. (Directions for cooking, page 28.) You can cook and even peel hard-boiled eggs the night before. If peeled, refrigerate in cold water overnight. Chomp on a piece of celery or raw carrot, too.

8. Granola. You can buy it. You can make it yourself (see below). Keep it in plastic bags in refrigerator or freezer. It makes a good on-the-move breakfast - or even lunch. Carry with you in a plastic bag.

+ + + + + + + + + + + + + +

+ GRANOLA +

Preparation: 10 minutes
Cooking: 40 minutes

"The olda
The Granola,
The betta
It getta."

True. Flavors mature and mingle. You thoroughly mix the dry ingredients, add liquids, bake. Then mix in dried fruit. Nutritionally, this is tops. Munch it dry, or eat as a cereal with milk. Or carry around for portable eating.

In large, shallow pan (roasting pan or 12" skillet is fine), combine:

1/2 box (1/2 lb.) regular oatmeal
1 cup wheat germ (regular or toasted)
1 small can shredded coconut
1 cup slivered almonds
1/2 cup soy flour
1/2 cup sesame seeds
1/2 cup millet meal
1/2 cup raw sunflower seeds

In a separate bowl, mix:

3/4 cup salad oil
1/2 cup water
1 1/2 teaspoons vanilla extract
1 1/2 teaspoons salt
1/2 cup honey

Pour wet ingredients over dry. Toss and mix well do dampen all. Bake uncovered in 325 oven about 40 minutes, stirring at least every 10 minutes. When baked and cooled, mix in 2 boxes dried mixed fruits (cut up larger pieces). Dried fruits are optional.

+ CHATTER +

1. You guessed it - an impossible recipe if there isn't a health-food store near you. But we'll bet there is; look again! These stores are burgeoning everywhere, on campus and off.
2. Keep leftover ingredients in the refrigerator until you make the next batch of Granola.
3. Of course, you can vary the ingredients, adding more of things you like, subtracting others.

+ +

+ OTHER BREAKFASTS +

Eggs might have been created just for college students. They're the perfect food. Cheap, fast-cooking, they contain more protein, pound for pound, than any other food. But they *are* easily offended. If you ignore them while they they're cooking on the stove top or cook them too fast with high heat, they get spiteful and promptly change to rubber. Eggs always vulcanize if not treated with respect. The scrambled variety seems to be best to have with bacon or sausage.

+ HARD-BOILED EGGS +

Put eggs in a saucepan, cover with *cold* water. (Cold water prevents eggs with unseen cracks from frothing over.) Cook over medium heat for 20 minutes. Immediately pour off hot water. Cover eggs with cold water to stop cooking and to prevent yolks from turning dark. Scratch them with a pencil for easy identificatoon in the refrigerator.

+ SCRAMBLED EGGS FOR TWO +

4 or 5 eggs
2 tablespoons butter or margarine
Salt and pepper

Open eggs into a mixing bowl, and beat with a fork or wire whisk for about 30 seconds. (Don't try any kind of electric beating gadget. Over-beaten eggs get a cheesy texture.) This will be very quick:

1. Heat butter in large skillet over medium heat. When it bubbles and coats the pan bottom, add beaten eggs. Cook for about 30 seconds.

2. Now, with a spoon, draw an asterisk * pattern through the eggs to allow raw part to run to the bottom and get cooked. Make the asterisk again, then gently turn over any uncooked egg so that it cooks. Remove eggs from heat before you think they're quite finished because they'll go on cooking anyway.

The eggs are now completely cooked but light and airy. They should lift out of the pan leaving it shiny clean. Add salt and pepper at the table.

+ FRIED EGGS +

2 eggs
1 tablespoon butter, margarine, or bacon grease

Over medium heat, melt butter in small skillet.

Open eggs into a cup. Slide eggs into hot butter. (The cup helps you place them more evenly in the pan.)

Let egg white harden for about 30 seconds, then cover pan with a lid. Trapped moisture under the lid steams the egg tops, cooking them. Serve in 1 minute, or when tops look right to you. Eggs should slide right out of the skillet. If not, use a spatula to get them out.

+ EGGS IN A CUP +

These are soft-boiled eggs (cooked white, soft yolk) mixed with broken up toast. They always taste good because the toast soaks up glop in case the eggs aren't cooked just right - which can happen because of different-size eggs.

2 eggs
1 teaspoon butter
1-2 slices toast
Salt and pepper

Make toast while eggs boil.

In a saucepan, cover eggs with cold water, place over high heat. Cook 6 minutes in all. Pour off hot water, hold eggs under cold tap water just a few seconds for easier handling.

Crack eggs into a cup or bowl. Scoop all white from shell with a spoon. Add butter, salt, pepper, broken-up toast. Mix well.

+ + + + + + + + + + + + + +

+ HOW TO COOK BACON +

Bacon varies enormously depending on how it is cured, how old, etc. All of it is expensive, considering that so much of the weight drains off into grease (but bacon grease is useful in small quantities; save it). Supermarkets often carry "country-style" bacon which they package themselves. It is cheaper than brand-name bacon and can be excellent. See if you can find a package with a lot of lean streaks. You already know bacon is good with pancakes, not just eggs, yes?

+ FRIED BACON +

The slices fry more evenly if cut in half. You can move them around more easily, avoid charred centers/raw ends. Just cook in a skillet over medium heat, drain on a newspaper or brown-paper bag. (Save bacon grease in a clean can. Refrigerate. Use to cook eggs and other things you'll come across in recipes.)

+ BROILED BACON +

You can broil it, but it makes a greasy mess in the stove. Forget it.

+ BAKED BACON +

Very good for a group. You don't have to watch this carefully and it's a good way to cook bacon in quantity when you're preparing other things.

Heat oven to 400. Stretch room-temperature bacon on wire rack in roasting pan or on broiler tray. Put in oven for about 12 minutes, depending on its thickness. Pour off grease and baked bacon turns into perfect, flat, crisp strips. When done, pat them between two pieces of brown paper to remove more grease.

+ + + + + + + + + + + + + + +

+ HOW TO COOK SAUSAGE +

There are a zillion kinds of sausage. We're talking about little pork or "link" breakfast sausage. Being made of pork, it must be cooked to well done because almost all pork contains microscopic, parasitic worms (!) which cause trichinosis - a Bad Disease.

+ BREAKFAST SAUSAGE, STEAM-FRIED +

Cut sausages apart. Place them in a skillet with about 1/2 cup of water (enough to barely cover bottom of pan). Cover pan. Simmer sausages for 8 to 10 minutes. This steams the meat to make sure it's done, gets rid of some fat.

Remove cover. Pour off water, or let it evaporate. Cook sausage, shaking pan, till meat is evenly browned. Drain on paper.

+ SUGGESTIONS FOR BRUNCH +

Plenty more brunch ideas under SUNDAY in each of the four weeks worth of menus that follow. But here are two recipes in the egg department.

+ FRENCH TOAST +

Use a large mixing bowl. The bottom should be wide enough to allow a slice of bread to lie flat. Beat together 1-2 eggs and 1/4 cup milk thoroughly, till well mixed. Stack 2 slices of bread in mixture. Turn until both sides of each slice are well soaked.

In large (12") skillet, melt 2 tablespoons butter over medium heat till bubbly. Add the soaked bread. After 2-3 minutes, turn bread in skillet with spatula, and brown other side. Meanwhile, soak 2 more slices in egg-milk mixture. Remove browned French toast to plate. Now fry last 2 slices in same manner. Top with maple syrup, honey, or jam, and serve with bacon or sausages.

+ PETER'S HANGOVER OVEN DISH +

Preparation: 15 minutes
Cooking: 30-40 minutes

Serves 8. This hearty casserole makes a cheap, superb brunch. A simple way to cook for a crowd and not blow your mind. You come up with a creation that melts in the mouth and is filled with lots of delicious surprises.

INGREDIENTS:

12 eggs
12 slices bacon
Butter
3/4 lb. old-fashioned store cheese
3 doorknob-size tomatoes (medium)
2 tablespoons Worcestershire sauce
1 teaspoon salt

PREPARATION:

Preheat oven to 350.

In skillet: Fry bacon crisp over medium heat, 10-15 minutes. Drain it on newspaper or paper bag.

While bacon fries: Thickly smear butter all over inside of 3-quart Pyrex casserole (borrow one).

Into casserole: Grate, on large holes of grater, the cheese. Slice and chop tomatoes. Add to casserole. Measure in Worcestershire sauce and salt.

Beat eggs till frothy in large mixing bowl. Add to casserole. Stir.

When bacon is crisp and drained, break into pieces into casserole. Stir till well mixed. Add 1 tablespoon butter, cutting into tiny nips and burying in mixture. Cover. (Lacking lid, use aluminum foil.)

Bake on middle rack in oven, door closed, for 30 minutes. Insert knife in casserole center to test: If it pulls out oily but without egg adhering, it's done. If not, give it 5-10 minutes more and test again.

+ CHATTER +

1. This is great with heated rolls, or French or Italian bread which has been wrapped in foil and heated in oven with casserole for 15 minutes.

2. Very important: Lacking the old-fashioned store cheese, or "rat" cheese, 3/4 lb. of mild Cheddar will substitute nicely. Don't use "processed" cheese - the kind that says "cheese food" in fine print somewhere on the label. Natural cheeses all taste better and are better for you.

+ + + + + + + + + + + + + +

+ +

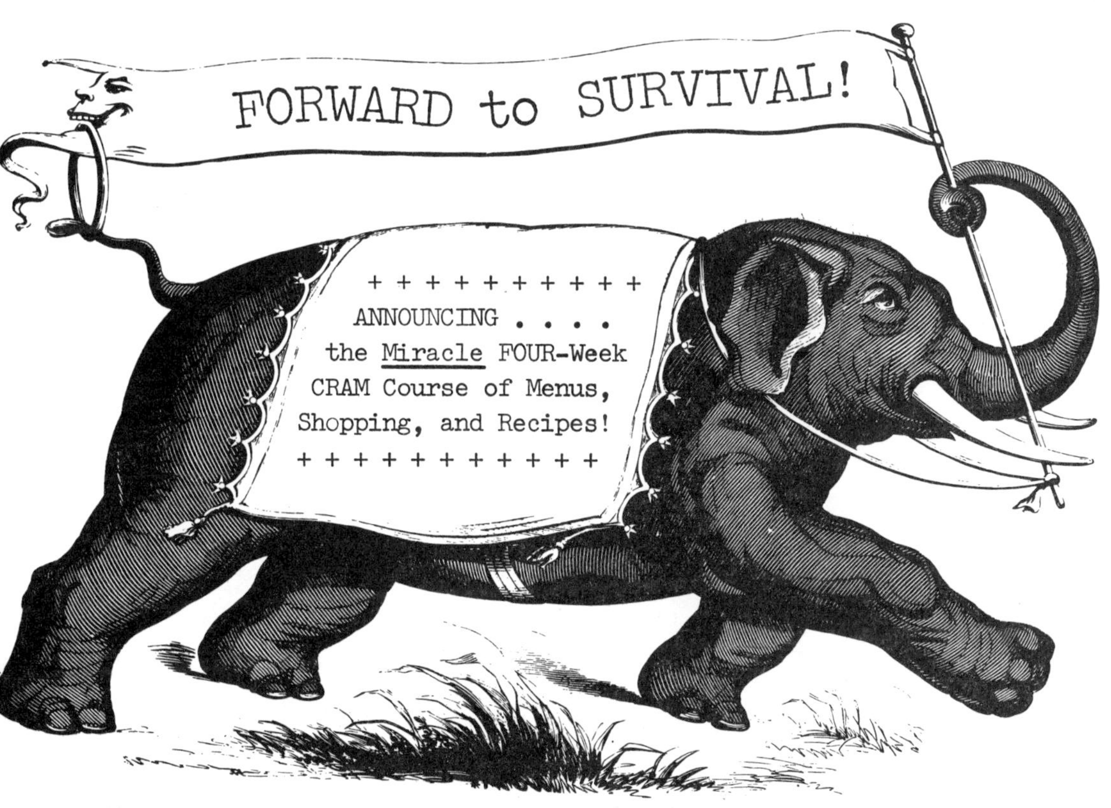
FORWARD to SURVIVAL!
+ + + + + + + + + + +
ANNOUNCING . . . .
the Miracle FOUR-Week
CRAM Course of Menus,
Shopping, and Recipes!
+ + + + + + + + + + + +

+ +

MENUS for FIRST WEEK

+ MONDAY +

Beginner's Chicken
Buttered Noodles
Green Peas

+ TUESDAY +

Broiled Chuck Steak Superstar
Baked Potatoes
Tomato with Onion & Mayonnaise

+ WEDNESDAY +

McCrystle's Survival Casserole
Tossed Green Salad with Sliced Cucumber
Traditional French Dressing

+ THURSDAY +

Roast Loin of Pork & Pan Gravy
Corn Pudding University of Virginia
Applesauce

+ FRIDAY +

Touchdown Tuna Casserole
Non-Harvard Beets
Salad Greens with Garlic French Dressing

+ SATURDAY +

Cambridge Glazed Roast Ham
Oxford Scalloped Potatoes
No-Place Buttered Broccoli

+ SUNDAY +

8 Suggestions for Ham Leftovers:

+ Brunch: Ham 'n' Eggs, Two Ways
A Good Guy's Western Omelet
+ Supper: Cold Sliced Ham on Rye
Quick Spreadable Ham Salad
Re-heated Ham Sweetooth
Tarzan Pea Soup
Actor's Hash

\+ +

Shopping - FIRST WEEK - Shopping

\+ +

BUY for MONDAY through SATURDAY (see CHATTER below):

\+ Meats +

2- to 3-lb. chicken fryer, quartered
1 1/2-lb. chuck steak, about 1" thick
1-lb. ground chuck
2- to 3-lb. pork loin roast
4- to 5-lb. pre-cooked ham, end or shank cut

\+ Fresh Vegetables +

7 Idaho baking potatoes
1 tomato (if in season; otherwise, buy canned sliced tomatoes)
1 green pepper
1 cucumber
1 head lettuce (romaine, Boston, or Salad Bowl)
1 bunch celery
1 bunch broccoli

\+ Canned Goods +

1 can peas (or pkg. frozen peas)
1-lb. can whole tomatoes
8-oz. can tomato sauce
8-oz. can whole-kernel corn
1 small jar applesauce
7 oz. can tuna
1 can cream of mushroom soup
1 small can or jar sliced beets

\+ Dairy Products +

8-oz. pkg. sliced American cheese
3-oz. mozzarella cheese

\+ Sundries +

1 pkg. noodles
1 box elbow macaroni
Bottle barbecue sauce (optional)
1 box wheat Melba toast

\+ CHATTER +

1. This is the shopping list for the MENUS for 6 days, to feed two. Not going to be cooking every night? Then, obviously, pare down the list. Don't have more meat in the refrigerator than you know you'll use.
2. Check this week's list of STAPLES below. You'll need those, too.
3. For SUNDAY. See suggestions for Sunday brunch and supper. Pick out recipes you want and add to your list ingredients underlined or listed there.
4. Need anything for any other meals? Remember BREAKFAST.
5. Between-meal SNACKS? Fresh fruits, fruit juices, ice cream, raw carrots and celery.

\+ STAPLES for FIRST WEEK + Do you have:

Milk
Butter or margarine
Eggs
Salt
Pepper
Instant minced onion
Garlic powder
Oregano
Prepared mustard
Dry mustard
Whole cloves (optional)
Sugar
Brown sugar
Flour (unbleached or stone-ground, if possible)
Wine or cider vinegar
Salad oil
Mayonnaise
Chicken bouillon cubes
Onions

Please! Always read to END of the day's recipes before you start.

+ +

MENU (serves 2)

Beginner's Chicken
Buttered Noodles
Green Peas

+ +

+ BEGINNER'S CHICKEN +

Preparation: 5 minutes
Cooking: 1 hour

This should really be called "Orientation Chicken," a step-by-step introduction to the fowl world. Easy and delectable, it's a foolproof way to arrive at broiled chicken - by baking it!

LINE UP YOUR INGREDIENTS:

2- to 3-lb. chicken (a fryer), quartered
3 tablespoons butter, or . . .
Bottle barbecue sauce (optional)
2 teaspoons salt
1/2 teaspoon pepper

PREPARATION:

Preheat oven to 350 (medium heat). (Close oven door.)

Wash your hands! Now wash chicken pieces quickly in cold tap water. Pat chicken dry with paper towels.

Place chicken pieces on rack in 9" x 11" roasting pan, skin side down.

Rub a bit of soft butter on each piece. Sprinkle with salt and pepper.

(If you prefer barbecue-sauce flavor to butter, generously pour it over each piece, coating them.)

Put pan on center rack of hot oven. Close door. Bake for 1/2 hour.

Take out pan. Reclose oven door to keep heat in.

Turn chicken over, skin side up. Repeat as before with butter and salt and pepper (or barbecue sauce).

Return pan to oven. Close door. Time for last 1/2 hour.

Turn oven off. If necessary, leave chicken in oven to keep warm till vegetables are ready.

+ CHATTER +

1. Chicken should be cooked, tender, and moist. If you like it browner and crispy, broil or "quick-brown" it: Move rack of electric-stove oven up to 7" from top heating element; or, move chicken pan down to broiler tray of gas stove, about 5" away from flame. Turn oven dial to "Broil." Leave door of electric oven ajar. Brown chicken for 3-4 minutes. Keep an eye on it. It burns fast, so take care.

2. Save all bones, even chewed ones, in plastic bag. Refrigerate. See Survival Bone Soup, page 142.

+ + + + + + + + + + + + + +

+ BUTTERED NOODLES + Takes 10 minutes

Noodles and such pastas, unless extra fine or very thick, usually take about 8-10 minutes to cook, in rapidly boiling water. We favor 8 minutes for the chewy effect. Overcooking makes them limp and gummy.

INGREDIENTS:

1 1/2 cups (4 oz.) broad noodles (any width)
3 cups boiling water
1 tablespoon butter
1/4 teaspoon salt

PREPARATION:

Start noodles 10 minutes before chicken is ready. In large saucepan, bring water to boil over high heat. Add noodles. When water boils again, time for 8 minutes. Don't cover pot! Taste. If done, take to sink, drain in sieve. Rinse under hot water tap. Return to saucepan. Add butter. Swirl with spoon. Salt to taste. Cover till ready to serve.

+ + + + + + + + + + + + + +

+ GREEN PEAS +

There is no mystery to vegetable cooking. Cook them over medium heat in very little water for very little time, until just tender. When done, never let them sit in the water to get soggy and lose vitamins. Drain them. Then drink the juice, or save it for your soup pot, whichever. But don't pour all that precious nutrition down the drain. The sink pipes are strong enough!

INGREDIENTS:

1 package frozen peas, or
1 can peas
1 tablespoon butter
Salt to taste

PREPARATION:

Cook peas when chicken is done and waiting in oven.

If frozen peas, follow directions on package. But it's preferred you use the salt after cooking. (Salt extracts vitamins during cooking.)

If canned peas, dump in small skillet (unless you own 2 saucepans). Heat through 4-5 minutes on medium heat. Drain. Drink juice. Return to skillet. Add butter. Mix to melt and blend.

DAY - First Week - MONDAY - First Week - MONDAY - First Week - MONDAY - First W

+ CHATTER +

1. If you buy and shell fresh peas, they will take 4-6 minutes longer to cook. Fresh vegetables usually take twice as long to cook as the frozen ones.

2. Wash and dry iron skillet. Then rub it inside with a drop of salad oil.

+ +

TUESDAY - First Week - TUESDAY - First Week - TUESDAY - First Week - TUESDAY -

+ +

Please, always read the WHOLE MENU before you start.

+ +

MENU (serves 2)

Broiled Chuck Steak Superstar
Baked Potatoes
Tomato with Onion & Mayonnaise

+ +

Preparation and cooking: 1 hour
Check next page and CHATTER.

+ +

+ BROILED CHUCK STEAK SUPERSTAR +

Today's meat is the quickest-cooking part of the meal. If possible, one hour before dinner, take it from refrigerator, unwrap it, and let it warm to room temperature on the rack in the roasting pan. After that, attend to your vegetables.

INGREDIENTS:

1 1/2 lb. chuck steak (1" thick)	Salt
1/4 teaspoon garlic powder	Pepper

PREPARATION:

When potatoes (next page) are baked, turn oven dial to "Broil."

Set rack about 7" from top electric heating element, or broiler tray 5" from gas broiler.

If outer area of steak is heavily fatted, trim off excess, but do leave at least 1/4" rim of fat. If you like garlic, sprinkle garlic powder on now. But if you're a purist, then . . .

Place steak in oven, as is. Do not season with salt prior to broiling. (Salt draws out the juices.)

Leaving electric oven door ajar, broil steak:

5 minutes on each side for rare
7 minutes on each side for medium rare
9 minutes on each side for well done

Dust lightly with salt and pepper. Serve at once, sizzling hot.

+ CHATTER +

1. If you have a steakboard with a "well" in it to catch the juices, carve on that. Otherwise a plate or platter with a rim (so the rich juice can't run all over the table) will do.

2. Timing varies with thickness of steak. Most oven-broiled steak should be at least 1" to 1 1/2" thick. Thinner than 1", the steak should be pan-fried in a hot skillet, 3-4 minutes per side.

3. Add today's steak bones to the bone bag in refrigerator. See Survival Bone Soup, page 142.

+ + + + + + + + + + + + + +

+ BAKED POTATOES +

If the only way you ever baked spuds was in the coals of a campfire, you're lucky. You hit the top! But, lacking glowing embers in your present digs, here's the other easy way to arrive at those soul-satisfying, buttery wonders.

TIMING:

Baking potatoes take 45 minutes to 1 hour, depending on thickness and oven heat. The ordinary Idaho potato - usually as thick as a doorknob, about 4" long - is best for baking.

PREPARATION:

Turn oven dial to 450. Close door to preheat oven. Wash 2 potatoes, rubbing well with hands. Dry thoroughly. Rub skins with a dot of salad oil, or any cooking grease to moisten. Place on rack in center of oven. Close door. Bake 45 minutes.

If potatoes were very cold to start, they may cook through more slowly. Test, by squeezing gently; if potato is tender and gives to the squeeze, it's done. If hardish, bake 15 minutes more. Remove from oven. Prick skin twice with fork to let steam escape. Wrap in foil till steak is broiled.

+ + + + + + + + + + + + + +

+ TOMATOES WITH ONION & MAYONNAISE +

Fix while potatoes bake. One medium-size (tennis ball) tomato is ample for 2 people. Slice it in 4-6 slices. Arrange on dinner plates.

One small-size (golf ball) yellow onion is fine here. But you don't need it if you don't happen to like onions. Peel onion. Chop it up (see page 24). Sprinkle over tomato slices.

Add a good dollop (1 teaspoon) of mayonnaise on each slice.

+ + + + + + + + + + + + + +

+ CHATTER +

1. Please note that in this meal as well as many others, the longest cooking time goes to the vegetables and not the meat. Therefore, you must often start the meal by cooking the "accompaniments" first.

2. Potato note: If you bake 4 instead of 2, you can use the extras Sunday night in Actor's Hash, thereby saving work and fuel bills. Refrigerate in skins.

+ +

WEDNESDAY - First Week - WEDNESDAY - First Week - WEDNESDAY - First Week - WEDN

+ +

Remember! Read IT ALL before you start.

+ +

MENU (serves 2)

McCrystle's Survival Casserole
Tossed Green Salad with Sliced Cucumber
Traditional French Dressing

+ +

Preparation: 15 minutes
Cooking: 15 minutes

+ +

+ McCRYSTLE'S SURVIVAL CASSEROLE +

This is variously known in different households as Dog Food Casserole, Train-wreck, or Alamo Stew and is a magnificent mess of 13 inexpensive ingredients. Besides being delicious and cheap, it can be splashed together in 15 minutes and cooks through in 15.

LINE UP YOUR INGREDIENTS:

1 cup (4 oz.) elbow macaroni
1 tablespoon butter
1 medium green pepper
1 lb. ground chuck
1-lb. can whole tomatoes
8-oz. can tomato sauce

1 tablespoon oregano
1/2 teaspoon garlic powder
1 tablespoon instant minced onion
1 teaspoon salt
1/2 teaspoon pepper
3 oz. mozzarella cheese
4 slices American cheese

PREPARATION:

Boil macaroni in 3 cups boiling water for 8 minutes in saucepan.

Meanwhile: Open cans of tomatoes and tomato sauce. Cut green pepper in half. Remove seeds. Slice and chop up. Slice mozzarella thin.

In largest (12") iron skillet, melt butter over medium heat. Add green pepper and chopped meat. Cook 4-5 minutes, stirring often, till meat is no longer pink.

Spoon in the whole tomatoes and about 1/2 the juice. (Save the rest for your soup pot or drink it.) Pour in tomato sauce. Add oregano, garlic powder, minced onion, salt and pepper. Stir 1 minute, breaking tomatoes into pieces.

When macaroni is ready, drain it into sieve at sink. Add macaroni to skillet mixture. Stir. Then cook 4 more minutes to blend flavors.

Top meat-macaroni mixture with slices of both cheeses. Cover skillet with lid. Cook 3 minutes. It's done when it gets gooey.

+ CHATTER +

1. This recipe should leave plenty for a hearty lunch tomorrow.
2. Don't forget to oil your skillet tonight after washing and drying.

+ + + + + + + + + + + + + +

+ TOSSED GREEN SALAD WITH SLICED CUCUMBER +

Make this before you tackle the main-dish casserole. Then it's all ready, crisp and cold, to be served pronto.

INGREDIENTS:

5-6 large romaine lettuce leaves
1 small cucumber

Wash lettuce in cold water. Dry well with towel. Break into bite-size pieces with fingers. Place in medium mixing bowl or salad bowl.

Slice off green cucumber skin. Now, on cutting board, slice cucumber thin, crosswise. Add to lettuce bowl. Refrigerate.

+ + + + + + + + + + + + + +

+ TRADITIONAL FRENCH DRESSING +

This dressing so often is tasteless because cooks don't take the trouble to learn the simple rule of "3-to-1." That means 3 parts oil to 1 part vinegar. Armed with this fact, you'll never miss.

INGREDIENTS:

1 tablespoon vinegar (cider or wine type)
3 tablespoons salad oil
1/2 teaspoon cold water
1/4 teaspoon salt
1/8 teaspoon pepper
1/4 teaspoon prepared mustard

In small mixing bowl, plop in mustard. Add salt and pepper. Add vinegar. Briskly stir together several seconds. Pour in salad oil and water. Using dinner fork, stir, blending well. Set aside to "age."

At serving time, stir well again. Pour over lettuce and cucs. Toss with 2 large spoons about 15 times till leaves are well coated with dressing.

+ CHATTER +

1. Preferred salad lettuces are: romaine, Boston, Salad Bowl, or any of the darker green varieties. Beware chicory and escarole - gourmet's delights, but on the bitter side.

2. Wine vinegar or cider vinegar are tastier in dressing than the plain white.

3. Which salad oil should you use? Peanut, sesame, safflower, or corn oil are preferred by nutritionists. Be warned: Always refrigerate! Oils can turn rancid rapidly, then taste, smell - and later make you feel - horrible.

4. Best prepared mustards are considered (by gourmets) to be "Dijon" from France; or use Gulden's, Mr. Mustard, or French's Mild Mustard.

+ +

THURSDAY - First Week - THURSDAY - First Week - THURSDAY - First Week - THURSDA

+ +

Reminder: Please read EVERYTHING through first.

+ +

MENU (serves 2 or 3)
Roast Loin of Pork & Pan Gravy
Corn Pudding University of Virginia
Applesauce

+ +

+ ROAST LOIN OF PORK +

Preparation: 5 minutes
Cooking: Depending on meat weight 1 1/2 to 2 1/2 hours

Although this is your first crack at a ROAST, you will soon discover how to blast the roast mystique, as no cooking could be simples. But do be sure your oven temperature registers correctly; see page 23. For a 2- to 3-pound piece . . .

Preheat oven to 325. (Close door.)

Wipe pork loin with paper towel. Cut off most extra fat. Salt and pepper all over lightly. Place on rack in roasting pan.

Put pan on center rack of oven. Close door. Roast 45 minutes per pound, i.e.: A 2-lb. loin roasts 90 minutes or 1 1/2 hours; a 3-pound loin roasts 135 minutes or 2 1/4 hours. (See CHATTER 2.)

+ + + + + + + + + + + + + +

+ PAN GRAVY + Takes 5-7 minutes

INGREDIENTS:

1 tablespoon pork fat
2 tablespoons flour
1 cup chicken broth (made by melting 1 chicken-bouillon cube in 1 cup hot water)

PREPARATION:

Pour off almost all pork fat from roasting pan, leaving 1 tablespoon.

Stir in flour. Mix well with fat. Stir 2 minutes over medium heat until brown but not burned.

Slowly add chicken broth. Stir till blended smooth with flour. Then let bubble gently 5 minutes, stirring now and then.

Right! It's gravy!

+ CHATTER +

1. Try to remember always pour excess fat into a can. It can wreck your sink drain, and the entire plumbing system, eventually.
2. A larger pork roast should be cooked 30-35 minutes per pound.
3. Leftovers? See Survival Bone Soup.
4. Who ever heard of pork without applesauce. Chill for 1 hour before serving, pour into a bowl, and sprinkle cinnamon on top.

+ + + + + + + + + + + + + +

+ CORN PUDDING UNIVERSITY OF VIRGINIA +

Preparation: 10 minutes
Cooking: 45 minutes

A fine, thick pudding which perfectly complements the pork loin. It is truly delicious, out of all proportion to the effort involved. This dish should be started an hour before the roast is done.

LINE UP YOUR INGREDIENTS:

1 cup (8 oz. can) whole-kernal corn
2 tablespoons butter
2 eggs
4 level tablespoons flour
2 cups milk
3 teaspoons sugar
1 teaspoon salt

PREPARATION:

Oven should be at 325.
Melt butter in small skillet.
In mixing bowl, beat eggs till frothy.
Drain corn at sink.
To beaten eggs add: Drained corn, flour, sugar, salt, and milk. Stir well. Add melted butter. Stir again.
Grease 1 1/2-quart casserole. Pour moisture in.
Place casserole beside roast in oven. Close door. Bake slowly (at 325) 40-45 minutes. Stir corn mixture from bottom 3 times during baking.

+ +
FRIDAY - First Week - FRIDAY - First Week - FRIDAY - First Week - FRIDAY - Firs
+ +

Reminder. Read EVERYTHING FIRST.

+ +
MENU (serves 2)
Touchdown Tuna Casserole
Non-Harvard Beets
Green Salad with Garlic French Dressing
+ +

+ TOUCHDOWN TUNA CASSEROLE +

Preparation: 10 minutes
Cooking: 30 minutes

This all-time favorite is simply three well-mixed ingredients which blend in cooking. It's as easy and inexpensive as it is good tasting. In a totally carefree way, you consume your desperately needed vitamin D which is so abundant in seafood.

LINE UP YOUR INGREDIENTS:

7-oz. can tuna
Butter or oil
3 stalks celery with leaves
6 slices wheat Melba toast, crushed
1 can cream of mushroom soup
1/4 cup milk

PREPARATION:

Preheat oven to medium (350). (Close door.)
With paper towel or fingers, throughly rub butter on the inside of 1 1/2-quart Pyrex casserole.
Chop celery on chopping board.
Crush Melba toast and add to casserole.
Open and add mushroom soup.
Open tuna, drain off liquid into sink. Add to casserole.
Add chopped celery and milk. Mix well, breaking up tuna pieces.
Cover casserole. Place in oven on center rack. Close oven door, and bake for 30 minutes.

+ CHATTER +

For variety, some other time try substituting cream of celery or cream of chicken soup.

+ + + + + + + + + + + + + +

+ NON-HARVARD BEETS +

Jar or can. They are tasty cold or hot. While not important nutritionally (except for the green tops of fresh ones which are loaded with vitamin A), still, beets do count and perk up a plate with their luscious juicy look and color.

If you prefer beets cold, just open the jar and drain or drink the juice. Arrange in mounds on plates.
If you've never tried it, experiment by draining them and adding to the salad bowl just before you add the dressing. A delicious variation.
Heated beets: Simply open the jar into a saucepan and warm on medium heat 5 minutes. Drain in sieve and serve. You can add butter.

+ + + + + + + + + + + + + +

+ GREEN SALAD WITH GARLIC FRENCH DRESSING +

Prepare this while the tuna casserole is baking.

Wash 5-6 large lettuce leaves (romaine, Boston) in cold water. Shake water off and dry well (with towel).
Break into bowl into bite-size pieces. Refrigerate.

Next make the dressing. This is simply your friend of last Wednesday, Traditional French Dressing, with the addition of garlic flavor and subtraction of the mustard.

INGREDIENTS:

1/4 teaspoon garlic powder
1/4 teaspoon salt
1/8 teaspoon pepper
1 tablespoon vinegar (wine or cider)
1 teaspoon cold water
3 tablespoons salad oil

In small mixing bowl or a cup, measure garlic powder, salt, pepper, and vinegar. Mix with a fork a few seconds.

Add water and oil. Mix with beating motion till blended. Set aside.

When casserole is ready, pour dressing over salad and toss well with 2 large spoons, 12-15 times. Serve.

+ +

SATURDAY - First Week - SATURDAY - First Week - SATURDAY - First Week - SATURDA

+ +

Reminder: Read THROUGH SATURDAY before you begin.

+ +

MENU (serves 2 or more)   Cambridge Glazed Roast Ham
Oxford Scalloped Potatoes
No-Place Buttered Broccoli

+ +

Timing, over-all: 2 1/2 hours

+ +

+ CAMBRIDGE ROAST HAM +

Preparation: Zero minutes

Today's meal is a classic weekend family dinner, which will last at least two days for 2 people. Note the preparation times. Though the menu seems elaborate, nothing takes more than 10 minutes to prepare. All the work is done by the oven. The ham, being pre-cooked, is truly child's play. The glaze on it is just about the most delectable, sneak-another-piece flavor ever concocted; it's as easy to make as mud pies.

BUY: A 4- to 5-lb. piece pre-cooked ham - ask for "end cut" or "shank cut."

PREPARATION:

Pre-heat oven to 275. (Close door.)

Wipe ham off with paper towel.

Line roasting pan with aluminum foil for easier clean-up later. Rest ham in it, fatty side up. (You don't need pan rack for this.)

Place roasting pan on center rack in oven. Close door. Bake 2 hours. (This is a warming through procedure. You will add the glaze and re-bake it later.)

+ GLAZE + Preparation: 10 minutes

While ham is baking in low oven, prepare this glaze. You merely stir, warm, and smear it.

INGREDIENTS:

1 tablespoon butter
1 1/2 cups brown sugar
1 tablespoon dry mustard
2 tablespoons flour
Some beer, fruit juice, or ginger ale (whichever you have around)
10 whole cloves (optional)

PREPARATION:

Melt butter in small skillet over medium heat.

Remove to counter. Stir in brown sugar, dry mustard, and flour. Mix. Heat 2 minutes.

Slowly, in small quantities, like 1/2 teaspoons full, pour in and stir the liquid. Stir after each addition of liquid, putting in about 2-3 tablespoons in all, till the mixture is soft but not runny - like putty or wet mud pies.

Put glaze aside till ham has warmed through.

+ Since you have nothing more to do for 2 hours, prepare Scalloped Potatoes now and let sit till baking time. +

After 2 hours, remove ham from oven. Turn oven up to 350.

Let ham cool 10 minutes.

"Score" the ham fat: Cut diagonal gashes across top of fat, making diamond shapes.

Insert a whole clove in center of each diamond (optional).

Now, smear glaze on top all over, and along sides, too, till ham is totally encased in sweet stickiness.

Return ham to oven's center rack position. Close door. Bake 30 to 45 minutes.

+ CHATTER +

You will have the ham and the potatoes in oven at same time for last 45 minutes of cooking. Turn the roasting pan sideways so both pan and casserole will fit on center rack. If that won't work, it's OK to bake the potatoes on a higher rack than the ham. Just be sure to cover the casserole; you want the potatoes to be juicy, not dried out. (Heat rises, remember? Therefore top of oven is hotter than lower down.)

+ OXFORD SCALLOPED POTATOES +

Preparation: 10 minutes
Cooking: 45 minutes

Maybe these are the world's most savory potatoes. They'll turn out to be creamy yet crisp layers of potatoes with the tang of onion and melted cheese throughout:

LINE UP YOUR INGREDIENTS:

3 huge potatoes (approx. 2 lbs.)
3 1/2 tablespoons butter
1/2 cup chicken broth (1/2 chicken bouillon cube and 1/2 cup water)
2 tablespoons instant minced onion
3 slices American cheese
Salt
Pepper

Be sure oven is at 350.
Using 1/2 tablespoon butter, smear insides of 1 1/2-quart Pyrex casserole.
Peel and slice potatoes thin as crackers, on cutting board.
Dissolve 1/2 chicken bouillon cube in 1/2 cup HOT water.
Over low heat, melt 3 tablespoons butter in small skillet.
Divide potatoes in 3 equal mounds. Start layering into casserole:
First: A thick layer of potatoes (first mound) on bottom.
Second: Sprinkle all over 1 tablespoon minced onion.
Third: Break up first slice cheese and scatter all over.
Dust lightly with salt and pepper.
Now, continue this layering till all potato mounds, onion, and cheese are used up, ending with the cheese on top.
Over all, pour the 1/2 cup chicken broth. Next pour the melted butter over all. Cover casserole. Set aside.
Last 45 minutes of ham-and-glaze baking, put covered potato casserole in oven with ham. Uncover for last 10 minutes.

+ + + + + + + + + + + + + +

+ NO-PLACE BUTTERED BROCCOLI +

Preparation: 3 minutes
Cooking: 8 minutes

Sold fresh in markets most of the year, this vegetable looks like a bouquet for the Jolly Green Giant's bride, and well it should, bursting as it is with vitamin A and iron. Cook it right. Reap great rewards:

Cut off tough stem bottoms of 1 bunch broccoli, leaving about 3" stems. Wash well under cold running water. Put in large saucepan in 1 cup boiling water. Cover. Lower heat to simmer. Cook 8 minutes, or till fork pierces stem. Drain. Save or drink juice.
Butter. Salt and pepper. Serve hot. (Please eat stems and tiny tender leaves you didn't cut off. They are always the greatest repositories of vital nutrients.)

It's your day of rest and maybe you want to cook like crazy and maybe you don't. These suggested recipes run the gamut - from slice-and-serve obvious to some real flavorsome cooking.

Sunday, most food stores are closed. You're already supposed to have shopped for what you want, but just in case, BEFORE YOU START one of these recipes, check refrigerator and staple shelf to be sure you have the ingredients underlined or listed.

+ +

8 Suggestions for HAM LEFTOVERS (serve 2)

BRUNCH:
1) - 2) Ham 'n' Eggs, Two Ways
3) A Good Guy's Western Omelet

SUPPER:
4) Cold Sliced Ham on Rye
5) Quick Spreadable Ham Salad
6) Re-heated Ham Sweetooth
7) Tarzan Pea Soup
8) Actor's Hash

+ +

+ HAM 'N' EGGS, TWO WAYS +

1) Cut 2 (1/2" thick) slices ham. In smaller skillet: Melt 2 tablespoons butter. Fry ham in it over medium heat 4 minutes. Turn over.

Now, in second skillet: Melt over low heat 1-2 tablespoons butter. Crack in 4 eggs (2 each). Cover. When whites are firm and yellows still soft (in 3-4 minutes), eggs are done.

Put ham on plates. With spatula, gently slide fried eggs onto ham. Serve with toast or English muffins.

+ + + + + + + + + + + + + + +

2) Cut 2 (1/2" thick) slices ham. Then dice small. In mixing bowl, beat lightly 4 eggs. (Famished? Make it 6 eggs.)

In skillet: Melt 2 tablespoons butter. Add ham. Stir 1 minute. Add eggs. Scramble ham and eggs together over medium heat till eggs firm up. Take out of pan right away. Serve with toast or English muffins.

+ + + + + + + + + + + + + + +

3) + A GOOD GUY'S WESTERN OMELET +

Included for Auld Lange Syne. This tasty version regularly was whipped up by a Columbia Quarterback, Class of '17. It was delicious 40 years ago when he concocted it, and it still is.

INGREDIENTS:

2 slices ham	4-6 eggs
1 green pepper	1 tablespoon butter
1 medium onion (handball size)	Salt
1 small clove garlic	Pepper

Chop up ham. Remove seeds from green pepper. Chop pepper. Also chop up onion and garlic. In mixing bowl, beat eggs till frothy.

Melt butter in skillet over medium heat. Add onion and garlic. Cook 3 minutes. Don't burn. (Stir often.) Add green pepper. Cook 2 minutes more. Add ham to warm through, 1 minute.

Pour in beaten eggs. Don't stir for 1 minute. Then give a quick stir around. Cover. Cook 3 minutes or till firm. Don't overcook.

With spatula, fold omelet in half, like a letter. Invert onto plate. Cut in half and serve. Superb with slices of tomato topped with a dab of mayonnaise.

+ CHATTER +

Did you know the reddish-turning green peppers contain twice as much vitamin C as the plain green ones? Pick out the ripened ones whenever available.

+ + + + + + + + + + + + + +

4) + COLD SLICED HAM ON RYE +

You hardly need to be told how to make ham sandwiches. But don't forget to buy rye bread. If you want a real pick-up, try adding sliver-sliced onion, or dill pickle, or slices of tomato and cheese. Remember to butter or mayonnaise bread generously.

+ + + + + + + + + + + + + +

5) + QUICK SPREADABLE HAM SALAD +

Chop 2-3 (1/2" thick) slices ham to pea-sized cubes. Add 2-3 stalks celery, chopped. Put in bowl. Add 2 fat tablespoons mayonnaise. You now have a very respectable ham salad to eat on lettuce, with or without making a sandwich of it.

+ + + + + + + + + + + + + +

6) + RE-HEATED HAM SWEETOOTH + Timing, in all: 20 minutes

As the name implies, your warmed ham will be sweet (and fruity).

Serve with last night's leftover potatoes. To reheat potatoes: Put them on center rack of pre-heated 300 oven for 20 minutes, covered. If you've already consumed them, the ham is good with rice (page 56).

Cut 2 (1/2" thick) slices ham. In larger skillet: Melt 2 tablespoons butter over medium heat. Add ham and 1 tablespoon of leftover ham glaze. Pour in 1/2 cup orange juice. (Pineapple juice is good, too.)

When bubbles appear, turn heat to low. Cover. Cook 5 minutes. Turn slices over. Cover. Cook 5 minutes more. Serve.

\+ + + + + + + + + + + + + +

7) + TARZAN PEA SOUP + Cooking: 2 1/2 hours

This savory thick soup is really a meal in itself. You should make it whenever you have a leftover ham bone. It's a filling supper with buttered bread and glasses of milk.

Put ham bone in a 2- to 3-quart saucepan. Add 4 cups water. Chop and add 1 huge yellow onion. Measure in 1 cup dried split peas. Bring to a boil over high heat, then turn to low. Cover. Simmer 2 1/2 hours. (Onion disappears.)

Ten minutes before serving, toss in 2-3 slices chopped ham if you still have some around. Soup reheats well if you make it ahead.

\+ + + + + + + + + + + + + +

8) + ACTOR'S HASH + Timing, over all: 1 hour

It's mostly ham - please forgive the pun. But it does come from a guy majoring in play-writing at Yale. A princely hash:

In saucepan, boil 2 medium-size potatoes, UNPEELED, in water to cover them, for 25 minutes. Drain. When cool enough to handle, peel off skins.

Meanwhile, cut 4 slices ham, and cube. Chop 1 medium onion.

In large skillet, melt 3 tablespoons butter. Add onion and fry 4-5 minutes. Add ham and potatoes. Stir. Cover and cook 10 minutes on medium heat.

Stir again, and press down firmly with spoon. Cover. Cook 10 minutes more. Season, if necessary, with salt and pepper.

Very good topped with a couple of fried eggs.

\+ CHATTER +

1. If you have leftover baked potatoes from last Tuesday night, use those, minus the skins, of course. Saves the 25 minutes boiling time.
2. The excellent reason you boil potatoes with skins on is to keep vitamins and minerals (C and iron) from "bleeding" away into water.

\+ +

CONGRATULATIONS! You have now SURVIVED for ONE FULL WEEK!

\+ +

MENUS for SECOND WEEK

+ MONDAY +

Oven "Fried" Chicken with Country Cream Gravy
Fluffy Rice
String Beans Salad with Italian Dressing

+ TUESDAY +

Budget Beef Stroganoff
Buttered Noodles
Chilled Canned Asparagus

+ WEDNESDAY +

Grandma's Hamburgers on Buns
French Fried Onion Rings
Tossed Greens with Survival Salad Dressing

+ THURSDAY +

ABC Irish Pork Chops
Broiled Peaches
Canned Corn

+ FRIDAY +

Don't-Clam-Up Spaghetti
Fresh Spinach Salad
Garlic Bread

+ SATURDAY +

U. of Penn. Roast Leg of Lamb with Pan Gravy
Roast Potatoes
Shanghai String Bean Casserole

+ SUNDAY +

6 Suggestions for Lamb Leftovers:

+ Brunch: Lamb Steaks 'n' Eggs
20-minute Heavenly Hash 'n' Eggs
+ Supper: Re-heated Lamb Slices
Bombay Lamb Curry
Lamb Grump
Bottoms-Up Barley Soup

Shopping - SECOND WEEK - Shopping

BUY for MONDAY through SATURDAY (see CHATTER below):

+ Meats +

3-lb. chicken fryer, cut up
1-lb. boneless chuck steak, 1" thick
1-lb. ground chuck
4 pork chops, center-cut, 1/2" thick
5- to 7-lb. leg of lamb (See CHATTER, page 35)

+ Fresh Vegetables +

1 head romaine lettuce
1 bag spinach
4 medium potatoes
Lemons (optional)
Bunch parsley

+ Frozen Vegetables +

1 box broccoli spears
1 box French-fried onion rings
1 box French-cut string beans

+ Dairy Products +

1 pint sour cream
Shaker of grated Romano or Parmesan cheese

+ Canned Goods +

1 can whole string beans
4-oz. can sliced mushrooms
1 small can peach halves
1 can corn (niblets or creamed)
2 cans minced clams (7 oz. each)
1-lb. can mixed Chinese vegetables
1 can French-fried onion rings
1 can cream of mushroom soup

+ Sundries +

1 box Uncle Ben's converted rice
1 pkg. noodles
1 box wheat Melba toast
4-6 hamburger buns
1 pkg. thin spaghetti (spaghettini)
1 small loaf Italian bread

+ CHATTER +

Be clear on how much of this shopping list you need - go back and read the CHATTER for shopping the FIRST WEEK on page 35. You need to check STAPLES below. Remember BREAKFAST. Remember fresh fruit for SNACKS or desserts. Shop in time for SUNDAY.

+ STAPLES for SECOND WEEK + Do you have:

Milk
Eggs
Butter or margarine
Salt
Pepper
Paprika
Vinegar
Salad oil (corn or peanut)
Flour (unbleached or stone-ground, if possible)
Bottled lemon juice (or fresh lemons)
Bouillon cubes (beef and chicken)
Worcestershire sauce
Chili sauce
Ketchup
Hellmann's mayonnaise
Prepared mustard
Dried thyme
Garlic powder
Garlic bulb
Brown sugar
Fresh celery

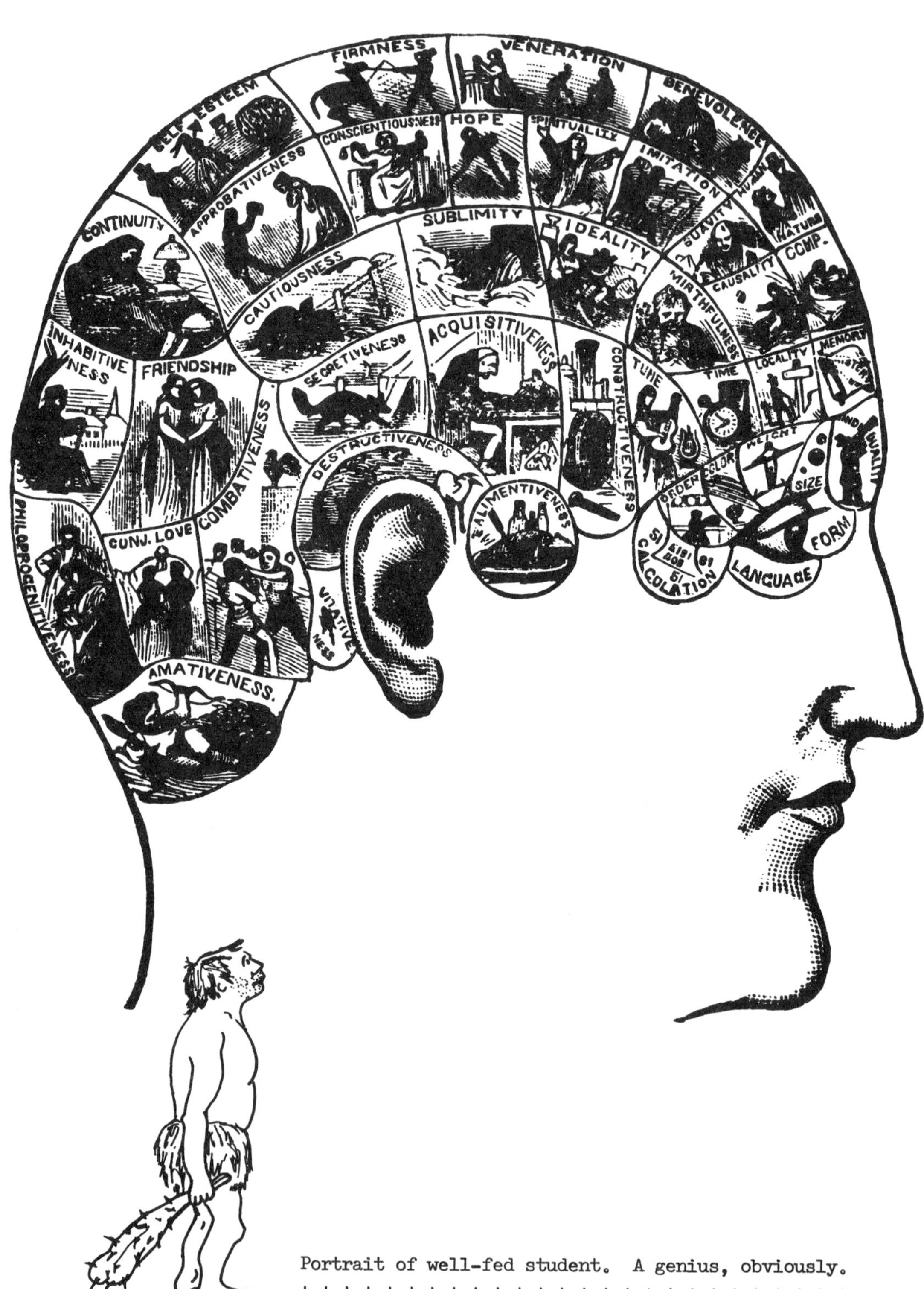

Portrait of well-fed student. A genius, obviously.

+ +

By now, you know you're supposed to READ EVERYTHING before you start. We won't pester you about this again.

+ +

MENU (serves 2)

Oven "Fried" Chicken with Country Cream Gravy
Fluffy Rice
String-Bean Salad with Italian Dressing

+ +

+ OVEN "FRIED" CHICKEN +

Preparation: 10 minutes
Cooking: 1 hour, 10 minutes

With this short-cut version, you'll produce a fine facsimile of Southern-fried chicken while avoiding the mess and indigestibility of deep-frying.

LINE UP YOUR INGREDIENTS:

3-lb. chicken fryer, cut up
Oil
3 tablespoons butter
1 cup flour
2 teaspoons salt
2 teaspoons paprika

PREPARATION:

If they're in the package, put aside innards (neck, gizzard, heart, liver) for later use. See CHATTER.

Rinse chicken quickly in cold tap water. Pat very dry with paper towels. Rub each piece all over with oil.

Melt butter in 9" x 13" x 2" roasting pan on top of stove, over low heat. Remove to counter.

Into medium-size paper bag measure flour, salt, and paprika. Shake one piece of chicken at a time in bag till well coated with mixture. Place chicken pieces, skin side down, in pan. Save flour mixture left in bag.

Bake in oven, uncovered, for 35 minutes. Open oven, turn all chicken pieces over, close door, bake 35 minutes more. (Start rice now.)

Remove chicken from pan to plate, and cover to keep warm. Make gravy.

+ COUNTRY CREAM GRAVY +

Takes 5-6 minutes

Place roasting pan over medium heat and slowly add 1 cup milk, stirring with a wooden spoon to scrape up all bits stuck to pan bottom.

Simmer, stirring constantly, till gravy thickens (5 minutes). If gravy doesn't thicken by then, mix in a glass 1 teaspoon each of leftover flour mixture and water to make a paste, and add to roasting pan. Simmer till gravy is thick enough. If needed, add 1/4 teaspoon salt. Serve over chicken and rice.

+ CHATTER +

1. Paprika sprinkled on meat to be baked or roasted adds a beautiful "browned" look and the taste is unobstrusive.

2. Save your $$. Make soup! After dinner, instead of throwing away the innards, put the neck, heart, and giblet (gizzard) into a saucepan with 3 cups of water, add all the chicken bones, even chewed ones. Add a large peeled onion, cut in half, and 2 chicken-bouillon cubes. Bring to a boil over high heat. Then turn down to simmer. Cook 1 1/2 hours, covered. Presto! Homemade chicken soup. Strain it. Save any chicken meat. Cut it up and return to pot. Add salt and boil 1/2 cup noodles in the soup for 8 minutes just before serving.

3. This soup, minus the noodles and chicken bits, is often referred to as "stock" in cookbooks. It is used to make sauces and other soups, and vegetables taste far better cooked in it rather than just in water.

4. Be sure to eat chicken liver for breakfast next day. Melt 2 teaspoons butter in small skillet. Put in liver, keep heat medium, shake liver around in butter. Turn in a couple of minutes. Cook couple of minutes more, till firm but still pink, not mud grey, inside.

+ + + + + + + + + + + + + +

+ FLUFFY RICE + Takes 25 minutes

3/4 cup Uncle Ben's converted rice
1 1/2 cups water
1 teaspoon salt
1 tablespoon butter

Follow package directions. OR:

Put rice in saucepan, add water and salt. Bring to boil. Stir once. Turn heat down to low. Cover.

Simmer 20 minutes, or till water disappears.

Add butter. Mix well. Serve.

+ CHATTER +

1. Rice is usually cooked 2-to-1, which means twice as much water as rice.

2. You note we specify Uncle Ben's converted. Outside of brown or unpolished rice (usually obtainable only in health stores), converted rice is the only kind that's good for you. The only kind. Good enough reason?

+ + + + + + + + + + + + + +

+ STRING-BEAN SALAD +

Before you even start your chicken, get the salad ready. It's so much better if you give it time in the refrigerator to think things over and get good and cold. Drain a can of whole string beans. Put them in a small bowl. Pour Italian Dressing over them. Refrigerate till dinner.

+ ITALIAN DRESSING +

1 clove garlic
1 tablespoon wine vinegar
3 tablespoons salad oil
1 teaspoon cold water
1/4 teaspoon salt
1/8 teaspoon pepper

You had this last week. Real garlic this time: Chop garlic very finely or mash (peel first). Put it in a cup. Add vinegar, oil, water, salt, and pepper. Stir briskly till blended. Pour over string beans. Refrigerate.

+ CHATTER +

1. The term for what's happening in the refrigerator to your string bean is "marinating." Many other items are marinated before cooking to improve flavor and texture.

2. Garlic is bought in bulbs. One "clove" means one section of a bulb. Most recipes call for 1-3 cloves, but there's one with 17! Garlic adds zest and flavor and is considered good for you, too. To remove its odor from breath, chew parsley. To remove odor from hands, use lemon juice, vinegar, or salt.

3. To chop, see page 24. But it really helps if you can afford a garlic press.

+ +

TUESDAY - Second Week - TUESDAY - Second Week - TUESDAY - Second Week - TUESDAY

+ +

+ +

MENU (serves 2)
Budget Beef Stroganoff
Buttered Noodles
Chilled Canned Asparagus

+ +

+ BUDGET BEEF STROGANOFF +

Preparation: 20 minutes
Cooking: 10 minutes

It's unlikely students at Moscow University sample much of this fare, but if they ever do, here comes another Revolution! This recipe is a direct descendant of Russian and Polish forbears, "Stroganoff" and "Smitane," meat-and-sour-cream concoctions that are quick to prepare and cook in a flash. Put canned asparagus in refrigerator well ahead to chill. The salad dressing above, minus garlic, would be good on it.

START THE BEEF:

1 lb. boneless chuck steak (1/2" thick)
3 tablespoons butter

Sharpen kitchen knife. Remove all fat from steak. Slice meat crosswise into thin slivers (1/8" thick). Cut slivers in half, lengthwise.

Melt butter in large skillet over medium-high heat. When bubbly, add beef strips. Stir around 2-3 minutes, or until all pink disappears.

Put beef on warm plate, pour skillet juices over it. Cover till sauce is ready.

MAKE THE SAUCE:

1 medium onion
4-oz. can sliced mushrooms
2 tablespoons butter
1 tablespoon flour
1/2 teaspoon salt
Dash pepper
2 teaspoons lemon juice
1 cup (1/2 pint) sour cream

Peel and halve onion. Run under cold water, then slice and chop it. Open can of mushrooms. Drain, saving juice for soup pot.

In same skillet as before, melt butter over medium heat. Add onion. Cook, stirring a bit, till onion is limp (2-3 minutes). Add mushrooms. Cook 1 minute more.

Sprinkle in flour. Stir 1 minute till browned. Add salt, pepper, and lemon juice. Stir 1 minute.

Spoon in sour cream. Cook 2-3 minutes, stirring often.

Now slide beef and juices into sauce. Turn heat to low. Stir around, then let simmer 4 minutes.

Cover and put to back of stove to keep warm. Serve over noodles.

Do noodles next.

\+ + + + + + + + + + + + + +

\+ BUTTERED NOODLES + Takes 10 minutes

Boil 4 cups of water in large saucepan. Add 2 cups (4 oz.) noodles.

Boil rapidly, uncovered, for 8 minutes. Drain. Rinse under hot tap water.

Return noodles to saucepan. Add 1 tablespoon butter and salt to taste. Mix well. Cover till broccoli is ready.

\+ + + + + + + + + + + + + +

After Monday and Tuesday's workout, this dinner is a SNAP.

+ +

MENU (serves 2)

Grandma's Hamburgers on Buns
French-Fried Onion Rings
Tossed Greens with Survival Salad Dressing

+ +

+ GRANDMA'S HAMBURGERS +

Preparation: 5 minutes
Cooking: 8 minutes or so

LINE UP YOUR INGREDIENTS:

1 lb. ground chuck
1 small onion
1 egg
1 1/2 teaspoons salt
1/4 teaspoon pepper
2 tablespoons butter or bacon fat
Hamburger buns

PREPARATION:

Slice and chop onion.

Break egg into medium mixing bowl and beat with fork, or wire whisk, till all is yellow.

Add onion, salt, pepper, and mix together. Add ground chuck and stir hard till all is mixed up.

Shape meat into 4-6 balls by hand, then flatten them to 1/2" thick with palm.

Melt butter, or bacon fat, in your largest skillet over medium heat. Put in hamburgers.

Fry 4 minutes on each side for rare burgers, turning once with spatula.

For medium rare, fry 5-6 minutes per side. For well done, 8 minutes on each side.

+ CHATTER +

1. For hamburgers, ground chuck is best. The most expensive cut (ground round) is a bit too dry and fatless (unless you're dieting), and the cheapest (ground beef or hamburger meat) is too fat and therefore uneconomical.

2. For extra-delicious flavor, some time substitute a packet of George Washington Beef Seasoning for the salt and pepper. Use 1 packet per each pound of meat.

3. If you've saved, and refrigerated, in a can your leftover breakfast bacon fat, hamburgers are even better cooked in that. Grandma said so.

4. Maybe this is more meat than you can eat. Save out a couple of uncooked patties, wrap in Saran, and freeze for a starving midnight. Or refrigerate to cook for BREAKFAST.

+ FRENCH-FRIED ONION RINGS +

Follow directions on 1 package of frozen French-fried onion rings. Some brands have 5-7 minute directions, others 10.

+ + + + + + + + + + + + + + +

+ TOSSED GREENS WITH SURVIVAL SALAD DRESSING +

A good big salad tonight. Make it ahead and refrigerate. Break up 4-5 large leaves of lettuce per person into bite-size pieces. Wash and dry well. Place in large mixing bowl. Make dressing ahead, too. This original recipe is creamy-smooth, with a nice tang.

INGREDIENTS:

3 tablespoons mayonnaise
3 tablespoons milk
1 tablespoon ketchup
1 tablespoon sour cream
1 teaspoon salad oil
1/2 small garlic clove, minced

Measure all ingredients into small mixing bowl, and mix together till well blended.

Pour over salad shortly before serving. Toss, mixing, 10-15 times.

+ CHATTER +

1. Hellmann's mayonnaise is best here.
2. Always refrigerate this dressing.

+ +

THURSDAY - Second Week - THURSDAY - Second Week - THURSDAY - Second Week - THUR

+ +

+ +

MENU (serves 2)

ABC Irish Pork Chops
Broiled Peaches
Canned Corn - Creamed or Niblets

+ +

+ ABC IRISH PORK CHOPS +

Preparation: 15 minutes
Cooking: 45 minutes

When Mike Mullen came from Ireland to Fordham, this was his total catalog of recipes. But, my, 't'was a grand one! So he passed it on to Mary, and she says this is how it goes:

LINE UP YOUR INGREDIENTS:

4 center-cut pork chops (1/2" thick)
1 large yellow onion
1 large clove garlic
1 teaspoon bacon fat or butter
Salt
Pepper

PREPARATION:

Scrape chops on both sides lightly with knife to remove any bone particles. Cut off extra fat, leaving a rim the thickness of a pencil.

Peel, slice, and chop the garlic and onion, using a chopping board.

COOKING:

A. In large skillet, melt butter or bacon fat over medium flame, and brown chops on each side, 5-7 minutes in all. Remove from skillet to a plate.
B. Put onion and garlic in skillet and let fry 3 minutes, till limp but not brown. Push onions to one side of skillet.
C. Return chops to skillet. Smother them with onions. Dust lightly with salt and pepper. Cover with lid and cook on low heat 45 minutes.

+ CHATTER +

1. For the last time! (Maybe.) Do rub your iron skillet with a drop or two of oil after you've washed and dried it thoroughly.
2. Add all pork-chop bones to bone bag in refrigerator.

+ + + + + + + + + + + + + + +

+ BROILED PEACHES + Takes 6 minutes

INGREDIENTS:

1 small can peach halves
1 tablespoon butter
2 tablespoons brown sugar
2-3 teaspoons sour cream (optional)

PREPARATION:

Lightly butter small skillet or small cake pan.

Drain peaches. Drink juice. Put peach halves in pan, cut side up. Sprinkle each half with brown supar. Dot tops of peaches with bits of butter.

Turn on broiler. (Place electric-oven rack 7" from top heating element.) Run peaches under boiler till brown sugar bubbles, 2-3 minutes.

Serve immediately with pork chops. Place a dab of sour cream on center or each peach. This is optional, but delicious - and convenient if you have a bit of sour cream left over from last Tuesday.

+ CANNED CORN + Takes 3 minutes

If creamed style: Turn into saucepan. Warm over low heat while peaches broil. It does not need butter.

If niblets: Turn corn and juice into saucepan. Warm over low heat while peaches broil. Drain in sieve. Add butter.

Cover to keep warm till dinner is ready.

+ CHATTER +

1. Although corn is low in vitamin content, it is not totally deficient. Therefore, save the juice - if you like the flavor - for your soup pot.

2. Oil your skillet after washing and drying. (Sorry! Just had to say it again.)

+ +

FRIDAY - Second Week - FRIDAY - Second Week - FRIDAY - Second Week - FRIDAY - S

+ +

+ +

MENU (serves 2)
Don't-Clam-Up Spaghetti
Fresh Spinach Salad
Garlic Bread

+ +

+ DON'T-CLAM-UP SPAGHETTI + Preparation: 10 minutes
Cooking: 10 minutes

A classic Mediterranean meal. The first forkful of clam spaghetti doesn't send you anywhere because it takes a few bites for the subtle flavors to accumulate. Then, ecstasy! Make the garlic bread and salad first, so you can sit right down the minute the sauce is ready. That takes about 10 minutes.

LINE UP YOUR INGREDIENTS:

1/2 lb. thin spaghetti
3 medium garlic cloves
1/2 cup chopped fresh parsley
2 cans minced clams (7 oz. each)
3 tablespoons butter
3 tablespoons oil
3 oz. (1/2 cup) grated Italian cheese (Romano or Parmesan)

Boil 8 cups of water. Add spaghetti. Boil 8 minutes, uncovered. Drain spaghetti at sink. Run under hot water. Leave in sieve.

Meanwhile: Chop up garlic cloves. Chop fresh parsley. Open cans of minced clams. Drain. SAVE JUICE!

In large skillet, melt butter over medium heat. Add oil. Add garlic and cook 1-2 minutes. Watch it. Don't let it burn.

Add parsley. Stir quickly. Add clam juice. Turn heat down to low and simmer, covered, for 5 minutes.

Add clams. Cook 1 minute more. Remove from heat.

Add cooked spaghetti. Stir well. Salt to taste. Serve at once. Top with grated cheese at table.

+ + + + + + + + + + + + + +

+ SPINACH SALAD +

Use a bag of fresh spinach. You'll only need half. Refrigerate remainder. Wash well (unless it's ready-washed). Dry thoroughly.

Break off stems and discard. Put spinach in large bowl. Add 2-3 stalks chopped celery (optional). Refrigerate.

Make Traditional French Dressing, page 41. Pour over spinach just before serving. Toss 15 times. Perfect with this meal!

+ CHATTER +

You will have another spinach recipe next Monday to use remaining half bag.

+ + + + + + + + + + + + + +

+ GARLIC BREAD + Needs 20 minutes warming

1 small loaf Italian bread (Hero-size)
1/2 stick butter
1 teaspoon garlic powder

Pre-heat oven to 350. (We're not reminding you to close oven door any more, either.)

Cut bread into 2"-wide chunks, 3/4 way through loaf, keeping bottom intact. Put on sheet of aluminum foil.

Melt butter in small skillet. Add garlic powder. Stir. Remove to counter beside bread.

Spread garlic-butter mixture generously between bread slices. Encase bread in foil.

Bake 20 minutes. Remove. Leave in foil till spaghetti is ready.

+ CHATTER +

1. Why not re-heated leftover garlic bread for breakfast tomorrow? Refrigerate in foil overnight.
2. To remove garlic odor from breath before class, chew parsley.

+ +

MENU (serves 2)

U. of Penn. Roast Leg of Lamb with Pan Gravy
(lamb lasts 3-4 meals)
Roast Potatoes
Shanghai String Bean Casserole

+ +

+ U. OF PENN. ROAST LEG OF LAMB + Cooking: About 3 hours

This princely meal creates itself, slow-cooking in the oven without a glance from the chef. All you need is an oven which registers heat properly; see page 23. There can be no guesswork or hit-or-miss about oven heat with roasts, or you'll have a very disappointing dinner.

LINE UP YOUR INGREDIENTS:

5- to 7-lb. leg of lamb	Salt
2 cloves garlic	Pepper
2 teaspoons lemon juice	Paprika

PREPARATION:

Remove lamb from refrigerator 1 hour before cooking.

Preheat oven to 325. (Close oven door. We're going to quit reminding you to do that, now, too.)

Wipe off lamb with clean damp paper towel.

With sharp paring knife: Peel garlic. Cut in slivers. Make deep blade-wide cuts in lamb, inserting a garlic sliver in each one while knife is still in meat, then pull out knife, holding down garlic with finger. Watch that finger!

Carefully dribble lemon juice over lamb on both sider. Dust lightly with salt, pepper, paprika.

Place lamb on rack in roasting pan. Put in oven on center rack. Roast 25 minutes per pound (2-3 hours, depending on weight of meat; see CHATTER 3 again.)

+ PAN GRAVY +

Turn off oven. Remove lamb leg to platter. Put back in oven to keep warm.

Pour off excess fat slowly from roasting pan; leave just enough to make a visible puddle in corner of tipped pan (about 4 tablespoons). Add 4 tablespoons flour. Stir over medium heat on top of stove. Add 4 cups beef broth. (Make beef broth by melting 4 beef-bouillon cubes in 4 cups HOT water. Or, use 4 cups Survival Bone Soup, if you've started it.) Cook over medium heat 5 minutes, stirring some, till thickened. Salt and pepper to taste.

+ CHATTER +

You make that much gravy because you'll use it for leftovers, as we'll explain for Sunday.

+ + + + + + + + + + + + + +

+ ROAST POTATOES + Takes 1 hour

Peel 4 medium potatoes (2 are extra for tomorrow). One hour before lamb is done, drop them into roasting pan. Be sure to roll them in the juices in pan bottom. After 30 minutes, turn potatoes over, and cook 1/2 hour more.

+ + + + + + + + + + + + + +

+ SHANGHAI STRING BEAN CASSEROLE + Preparation: 5 minutes
Cooking: 45 minutes

1 pkg. frozen string beans, French-cut
1-lb. can mixed Chinese vegetables
1 can French-fried onion rings
1 tablespoon butter
1 can cream of mushroom soup
Salt, pepper

Follow directions on package of string beans, but cook for only a short time, as you want them crisp and green. Drain.
Grease inside of casserole with butter (or use large skillet).
Add drained string beans, drained Chinese vegetables, onion rings, and cream of mushroom soup. Add salt and pepper lightly.
Stir all around till thoroughly mixed. Cover.
Bake 45 minutes in 325 oven, along with leg of lamb.

+ + + + + + + + + + + + + +

If your sweet tooth is aching, try a dessert, Flaming Bananas on page125. It's great after roast lamb.

SUNDAY - Second Week - SUNDAY - Second Week - SUNDAY - Second Week - SUNDAY - S

It's that day again. Depending on how weary and/or hungry you are, try any of the following:

\+ +

6 Suggestions for LAMB LEFTOVERS (serve 2)

BRUNCH:	1) Lamb Steaks 'n' Eggs (Starved)
	2) 20-Minute Heavenly Hash 'n' Eggs (Also Starved)
SUPPER:	3) Re-heated Lamb Slices (Weary)
	4) Bombay Lamb Curry (Getting Up Steam)
	5) Lamb Grump (Fulla Beans!)
	6) Bottoms-Up Barley Soup (Broke)

\+ +

1) + LAMB STEAKS 'N' EGGS +

This is the recipe for the 2 uncooked lamb steaks you have in the refrigerator.

Put them on rack of roasting pan. Turn oven dial to "Broil." (Raise rack of electric-stove oven to within 7" of top heating element.)

Cook lamb steaks as you did the chuck steak, TUESDAY, First Week. If you like them pink inside, 6 minutes on each side is enough. Better done, 8 minutes per side.

These are great served with scrambled eggs (page 29).

\+ + + + + + + + + + + + + + +

2) + 20-MINUTE HEAVENLY HASH 'N' EGGS +

Chop fine: 3 (1/2" thick) slices cooked lamb, 1 huge yellow onion, 2 leftover roast potatoes.

In large skillet, melt 3 tablespoons butter over medium heat. Plunk in chopped lamb, onion, and potatoes. Sprinkle in 1/4 teaspoon garlic powder, and dust with salt and pepper.

Stir to mix all. Press flat in pan. Fry 10 minutes. Turn, like a pancake, with spatula, and press down again. Cover, and cook 10 minutes more.

Meanwhile, fry 4 eggs in second skillet (page 29). Put hash on plates. Gently top with fried eggs.

\+ + + + + + + + + + + + + + +

3) + RE-HEATED LAMB SLICES +

Simply slice off 4 generous (1/4" thick) pieces cooked lamb, put them into a skillet. Thickly slice in yesterday's potatoes, and pour pan gravy over all. Heat on medium for 10 minutes. As they say, better the second night!

Serve on toast, and you've made HOT LAMB SANDWICHES.

\+ + + + + + + + + + + + + + +

4) + BOMBAY LAMB CURRY + Preparation: Under 30 minutes

Cut up 4 cooked lamb slices into generous bite-size pieces. Coarsely chop a large onion and 1 garlic clove.

Melt 2-3 tablespoons butter in largest skillet. Add chopped onion and garlic. Cook over medium heat for 5 minutes. Then sprinkle in 1 tablespoon flour, and 1 teaspoon curry powder. (Some like it HOT. More curry powder?) Stir and cook together 1 minute more.

Add 1 1/2 cups lamb pan gravy (or 1 bouillon cube melted in 1 cup hot water). When it boils, add lamb pieces. Cover. Turn heat to low. Cook gently for 15-20 minutes.

Meanwhile, put on 1 cup Uncle Ben's converted rice to cook in 2 cups boiling water for 20 minutes (page 56). Serve lamb curry over the rice.

+ + + + + + + + + + + + + +

5) + LAMB GRUMP +

A 30-minute Western bean casserole dish. The basis of it is just 3 cans.

Preheat oven to 350.

Open and drain a 1-lb. can cooked pinto or white beans and a can of corn niblets. Open a can of cream of tomato soup.

Rub large skillet with 1 tablespoon butter. Dump in beans, corn, soup. Add 3 slices of cooked lamb cut into large bite-size pieces.

Next measure in 1 tablespoon instant minced onion and 1 teaspoon basil. If any roast potatoes are left, slice them thickly into skillet. Mix well. Slices of mild cheese (such as American) are nice on top, but not necessary.

Cover skillet. Bake 30 minutes.

+ + + + + + + + + + + + + +

6) + BOTTOMS-UP BARLEY SOUP + Cooking: 2 1/2 hours

This is what you do with the lamb bone. It's a filling, gently-flavored soup, thick as a Scottish porridge.

Cut meat off the bone. Put bone in largest saucepan. Add 1/2 cup barley and 8 cups water. Bring to boil. Turn heat to low. Cover. Cook 2 hours.

Add 2 thin-sliced carrots, 1 chopped onion, and 2 slices of diced lamb. Cook 1/2 hour more. Season to taste with about 2 teaspoons salt, 1/4 teaspoon pepper.

+ +

If you've made it this far, you're getting to be A PRETTY GOOD COOK!

+ +

+ +

MENUS for THIRD WEEK

+ +

\+ MONDAY +

Fiji Chicken Casserole
Oriental Browned Rice
Savory Spinach

\+ TUESDAY +

Quicky Swiss Steak
Potted Vegetables

\+ WEDNESDAY +

Spaghetti with Meat Sauce
Tossed Green Salad, Package Dressing

\+ THURSDAY +

Gourmet Pork Chops Gehrecke
Buttered Whole Hominy
Italian Squash

\+ FRIDAY +

Small Fry Fish
Boiled Potatoes
Grilled Tomatoes

\+ SATURDAY +

Budget Beef Roast, Au Jus
Pan-Roasted Potatoes
Herbed Green Peas and Celery

\+ SUNDAY +

6 Suggestions for Beef Roast Leftovers:

\+ Brunch: Roast Beef Hash 'n' Eggs
Steak 'n' Eggs with Onions

\+ Supper: Simple Reheated-Beef Sandwiches
Beef Slices Barbecued
Wetback Stew
Hearty Beef Soup

+ +

Shopping - THIRD WEEK - Shopping

+ +

BUY for MONDAY through SATURDAY (see CHATTER, page 35):

+ Meats +

2 1/2- to 3-lb. chicken fryer, cut up
1 1/2-lb. chuck steak, 1/2" thick
1/2-lb. chopped chuck
4 pork chops, center-cut, 1/2" thick
1 pkg. frozen fish fillets (flounder, halibut, sole, whiting) or, 1-lb. fresh fish fillets
4- to 6-lb. chuck roast (or "block chuck," "standing clod," or "rump roast")

+ Vegetables +

1 onion (or instant minced onion)
Fresh spinach from last week, or 1 pkg. frozen spinach
2 carrots
12 medium potatoes
Garlic
1 small head Boston or Bibb lettuce
3-4 zucchini (small green squash)
2 small tomatoes
Celery
1 pkg. frozen peas

+ Canned Goods +

1 can Campbell's cream of mushroom soup
1 can Campbell's cream of celery soup
1 can Campbell's consomme
1 can Campbell's onion soup
1-lb. can or jar meatless spaghetti sauce (Ragu, Boy-ar-dee, or Prince)
1-lb. can whole hominy

+ Dairy Products +

Shaker of grated Romano or Parmesan cheese (optional)
Butter or margarine
Eggs
Milk

+ Sundries +

1-lb. pkg. thin spaghetti (spaghettini)
1 pkg. Good Seasons salad dressing mix ("Italian," "Old Fashioned French," "Parmesan")
1 small can frozen orange juice

+ STAPLES for THIRD WEEK + Do you have:

Salt
Pepper
Salad oil (peanut or corn)
Vinegar (wine or cider)
Flour (unbleached or stone-ground, if possible)
Uncle Ben's converted rice
Bacon
Beef bouillon cubes
Lemon juice (Real Lemon)
Mayonnaise
Curry powder
Garlic powder
Oregano
Paprika
Basil or thyme

+ + + + + + + + + + + + + +

+ +

MENU (serves 2-3)

Fiji Chicken Casserole
Oriental Browned Rice
Savory Spinach

+ +

+ FIJI CHICKEN CASSEROLE +

Preparation: 5 minutes
Cooking: 1 1/2 hours

This may be the best recipe in the book. It has an exotic flavor, is excellent for parties, inexpensive, quick to prepare, and produces tender chicken and its own rich gravy.

LINE UP YOUR INGREDIENTS:

2 1/2- to 3-lb. chicken, cut up (a fryer)
Some butter or oil
1 can Campbell's cream of mushroom soup
1 can Campbell's cream of celery soup
1 1/2 teaspoons curry powder
1/2 teaspoon garlic powder (optional)

PREPARATION:

Preheat oven to 350.

Wash chicken quickly under cold water tap. Dry well.

Grease (with oil or butter) the large (12") skillet. Place cut-up chicken in skillet, skin-side up.

Open both cans of soup. Plop them onto chicken. Sprinkle in curry powder and garlic powder (optional). Mush soups around till all flavors blend and chicken pieces are completely covered with the mixture.

Cover skillet. Bake on center rack of oven for 1 1/2 hours. Last 1/2 hour of cooking time, remove skillet lid to brown. Start Browned Rice then.

+ CHATTER +

To reheat for a leftover lunch: Warm, covered, in a 300 oven for 20 minutes to 1/2 hour.

+ + + + + + + + + + + + + + +

+ ORIENTAL BROWNED RICE +

Preparation: 5 minutes
Cooking: 20 minutes

Here's rice that's firm and chewy, with a nutlike flavor and texture, and so good it can be eaten all alone. It's sometimes called rice pilaf.

LINE UP YOUR INGREDIENTS:

3/4 cup Uncle Ben's converted rice
2 tablespoons butter or oil
1 medium onion, or 1 1/2 tablespoons instant minced onion
1 can Campbell's consomme

PREPARATION:

Chop up onion. Melt butter in saucepan over medium heat. Add chopped onion. Cook, stirring a bit, for 3 minutes.

Add rice. Stir till well-coated, 1-2 minutes. Add consomme. Bring to boil over high heat.

Turn heat to low. Cover pan. Simmer 20 minutes. Serve.

+ CHATTER +

If you use instant minced onion, proceed the same way, but watch it, as it burns quickly.

+ + + + + + + + + + + + + +

+ SAVORY SPINACH + 12 minutes, total

A great flavor, and something easy to do with that leftover 1/2 bag of fresh spinach from last week. It also works with a defrosted package of frozen spinach.

LINE UP YOUR INGREDIENTS:

1/2 bag fresh spinach
2 tablespoons butter or oil
1 clove garlic
1/4 teaspoon salt

PREPARATION:

If you prefer chopped spinach to whole-leaf, cut it up now on wooden surface; otherwise, leave as is. (Is it sandy? Wash it.)

Peel and cut up garlic. In small skillet, melt butter over medium heat. Add cut-up garlic. Saute (fry) 2-3 minutes.

Add spinach. Cook, stirring and turning often, for 2-3 minutes, till limp, but not a sodden mass. Sprinkle in salt. Serve.

+ + + + + + + + + + + + + +

+ +

MENU (serves 2) — Quicky Swiss Steak with Potted Vegetables

+ +

+ QUICKY SWISS STEAK +

A meal-in-one-pot, this superb recipe manages to reach perfection in the shortest possible time, and is especially satisfying on a cold wintery night.

LINE UP YOUR INGREDIENTS:

1 1/2 lb. chuck steak (1/2" thick)
2 medium carrots
2 medium potatoes
1/2 teaspoon pepper
2 tablespoons flour
3 tablespoons bacon fat or butter
1 clove garlic
1 can Campbell's onion soup
1/2 can water
Salt

PREPARATION:

Wash carrots. Cut in 2" pieces. Peel potatoes. Cut in half, lengthwise.

Put steak on large sheet of wax paper (to avoid messy clean-up later). Sprinkle both sides of steak with pepper. Put 1 tablespoon flour on steak and spread around. Then, with back of spoon, press flour into steak till absorbed. Turn steak and repeat with second tablespoon flour.

Melt bacon fat or butter in large (12") iron skillet over medium heat. Add steak to skillet. Brown 3 minutes each side.

Add garlic, cut up. Saute (fry) 1-2 minutes.

Add soup, water, carrots, and potatoes.

Cover skillet. Bake in oven on center rack for 1 hour. Uncover for last 15 minutes. Salt lightly. Serve.

+ CHATTER +

If you're a vegetable maniac, when you put in the carrots and potatoes, you could also add some halved stalks of celery, a small turnip peeled and cut up, and any other hard vegetable you have around.

+ + + + + + + + + + + + + + +

That's it for today!

+ +

MENU (serves 2) — Spaghetti with Meat Sauce
Tossed Green Salad, Package Dressing

+ +

+ SPAGHETTI WITH MEAT SAUCE +

Preparation: 10 minutes
Cooking: 30 minutes

Anytime a crowd gathers, you can double or triple this and have a hit without destroying your bank account. But even when you're alone, this is good. It's zesty fare that sticks to the ribs.

LINE UP YOUR INGREDIENTS:

2 cloves garlic
3 tablespoons oil (peanut, corn)
1 1/2 teaspoons oregano
1/2 lb. chopped chuck
1-lb. can or jar meatless spaghetti sauce (Prince, Ragu, Chef Boy-ar-dee)
1/2 lb. thin spaghetti
Some butter
3 oz. grated Romano cheese (optional)

MAKE MEAT SAUCE:

Peel and cut up garlic cloves. In large (12") iron skillet, warm oil over medium heat 1-2 minutes. Add garlic. Cook 1 minute.

Add oregano. Stir around 1 minute.

Add chopped chuck. Stir till pink disappears.

Open and add prepared spaghetti sauce. Bring to a bubble over high heat. Turn to low. Cover skillet. Simmer 20 minutes.

COOK SPAGHETTI:

Now: Boil 2 quarts (8 cups) water in large saucepan. When boiling wildly, add spaghetti. Push down into water.

When water boils again, cook uncovered, 8 minutes, stirring occasionally. Test for doneness. Chew a strand.

Drain spaghetti at sink. Pour into skillet with sauce. Add a lump of butter. Stir around.

Cover. Simmer 10 more minutes. Serve topped with grated cheese or plain.

+ + + + + + + + + + + + + +

+ TOSSED GREEN SALAD, PACKAGE DRESSING + 5 minutes

INGREDIENTS:

1 small head Boston or Bibb lettuce (just enough for 2 people)
1 package Good Seasons Salad Dressing Mix ("Old Fashioned French," "Parmesan," or "Italian" are all good)
Cider or wine vinegar
Salad oil (peanut or corn)

PREPARATION:

Wash lettuce gently. Dry well. Tear into bite-size pieces.

Good Seasons Salad Dressing Mix comes with a free bottle. Directions for mixing proportions of vinegar, water, oil, and the package of spices are stamped on bottle. Follow them. Shake well.

Measure 2-3 tablespoons of dressing over lettuce. Mix 15 times till all leaves are well coated. Serve.

+ CHATTER +

Refrigerate remaining salad dressing. Shake each time before using.

+ +

THURSDAY - Third Week - THURSDAY - Third Week - THURSDAY - Third Week - THURSDA

+ +

+ +

MENU (serves 2)

Gourmet Pork Chops Gehrecke
Buttered Whole Hominy
Italian Squash

+ +

+ GOURMET PORK CHOPS GEHRECKE +

Preparation: 5 minutes
Cooking: 45 minutes

Frank Gehrecke, at Northwestern, handed us this winner. Here are plain old pork chops gussied up and tasting like $9.00 a plate. Their Grand Marnier (that's a liqueur) flavor is created by the addition of orange juice.

LINE UP YOUR INGREDIENTS:

4 pork chops (center cut), 1/2" thick
1 teaspoon salt
1/2 teaspoon pepper
1/2 cup flour
3 tablespoons butter
2 cups orange juice

PREPARATION:

Scrape both sides of chops lightly with knife to remove tiny bone particles. Cut off excess fat, leaving a 1/8" rim.

In paper bag mix: salt, pepper, and flour. Shake each chop in bag till coated with mixture.

Melt butter in large (12") skillet over medium heat. Brown chops in skillet, 5 minutes each side.

Add 1 1/2 cups of the orange juice. Bring to a boil on high heat. Turn heat down to low. Simmer chops uncovered for 45 minutes.

+ CHATTER +

1. If too much orange juice evaporates while cooking, add 1/2 cup more. You should expect to end up with 1/2 to 3/4 of orange sauce in the skillet from the juice.

2. You are advised here to buy center-cut pork chops because, though not the cheapest, they're the best buy, having the least fat and bone.

+ + + + + + + + + + + + + +

+ BUTTERED WHOLE HOMINY + Total time: 12-15 minutes

This is not the Southern "grits" which many Northerners find unappealing (!), but kernels of hard corn with the hulls removed. A nice flavor, good solid texture.

LINE UP YOUR INGREDIENTS:

1-lb. can whole hominy
2-4 tablespoons bacon grease or butter
Salt and pepper

Open hominy can, drain liquid into sink.

Heat 2 tablespoons bacon grease in smaller skillet over medium heat. Add drained hominy. Stir.

Let hominy saute slowly (adding a little more grease if it sticks) until kernels are dryer, well separated, and somewhat browned. Stir often. Add salt and pepper. Serve.

+ + + + + + + + + + + + + +

+ ITALIAN SQUASH +

Preparation: 5 minutes
Cooking: 20 minutes

You start this while the pork chops are simmering, and when it's done you'll understand why Italians sing whole operas in praise of vegetables.

LINE UP YOUR INGREDIENTS:

3-4 slim zucchini (green squash), 6" long
3 tablespoons oil
2 cloves garlic
Salt to taste

PREPARATION:

Under tap water, wash zucchinis well, rubbing hard. Remove zucchini stems. Slice into 1" chunks. Peel and slice garlic.

In saucepan, warm oil over medium heat. Add zucchini and garlic together. Cook till squash browns a bit on both sides, about 5 minutes.

Cover saucepan. Turn heat to low. Simmer 15 minutes more. Dust lightly with salt. Serve.

+ +

FRIDAY - Third Week - FRIDAY - Third Week - FRIDAY - Third Week - FRIDAY - Thir

+ +

+ +

MENU (serves 2)

Small Fry Fish
Boiled Potatoes
Grilled Tomatoes

+ +

+ SMALL FRY FISH +

Preparation: 1 minute
Cooking: 5 minutes

A word in defense, and in honor, of our aquatic friend, the Fish, which has been the entire protein staple of many countries through the ages. This finny fellow contains about the same amount of protein as meat, yet frequently is much cheaper. As bonuses, fish supplies generous amounts of vitamin A, phosphorus, and iodine. Also, being fairly fat-free, it cooks quickly and fills you up without fattening you. Fish has one secret: Cook for a short time, over gentle heat. For this menu, start potatoes and tomatoes before fish.

LINE UP YOUR INGREDIENTS:

1 package frozen fish fillets (flounder, halibut, sole, whiting)
or
1 lb. fresh fish fillets (turbot from Greenland is cheap & good)

Salt
Paprika
1 tablespoon butter
1 tablespoon oil
Lemon juice (optional)
Mayonnaise (optional)

PREPARATION:

If frozen: Defrost slowly at room temperature, according to package instructions.

Spread fish fillets on flat counter surface. Lightly sprinkle both sides with salt and paprika.

In large (12") skillet: Melt butter and oil together over medium heat, till bubbling. Gently lay fish fillets in skillet. Cook 3 minutes.

Turn with spatula. Cook 2-3 minutes more. Fish doneness test: If you can separate (flake) a piece easily with a fork, it's cooked.

Put on warm plates to serve. If you like, bless each fillet with a few drops of lemon juice and a dollop of mayonnaise, and serve at once. But it's just as good plain.

+ CHATTER +

1. Fish of the sea contain iodine. Trout, perch, etc., do not.
2. In frying, the combination of butter plus oil prevents burning.
3. Fish fillets are also good sprinkled first with flour or covered thickly with wheat germ before frying. In fact, the second way is absolutely marvellous!

+ + + + + + + + + + + + + +

+ BOILED POTATOES + Cooking: 30-40 minutes

About the same calorie count as an equal-size apple, and full of vitamins B, C, iron and other minerals - IF cooked properly!

PREPARATION:

Cook 4 medium-size potatoes in enough boiling water to cover them.

After 30 minutes, test for doneness by stabbing one with a fork. If fork penetrates easily, they're cooked. If not, boil 10 minutes more. Drain at sink.

How to peel a hot potato skin and save your own: Spear a potato with kitchen fork. Hold aloft, and peel with sharp knife. If thoroughly cooked, the jacket will slip off easily.

Return potatoes to saucepan; cover till dinner's ready. Good plain, or with salt, pepper, and gobs of butter.

+ + + + + + + + + + + + + +

+ GRILLED TOMATOES + Takes 3-5 minutes

INGREDIENTS:

2 small tomatoes
Oil
1 teaspoon basil
Salt & pepper

PREPARATION:

Turn oven to broil.

Oil small skillet. Cut tomatoes in half. Place them in skillet, cut side up up. Sprinkle salt, pepper, and 1/4 teaspoon basil on each slice.

Broil on rack, 7" from heating element, till browned and bubbly, or 3-5 minutes. Turn broiler off. Leave tomatoes in oven to keep warm till fish is ready.

+ CHATTER +

Extra potatoes can be saved and fried for Sunday leftovers.

+ +

SATURDAY - Third Week - SATURDAY - Third Week - SATURDAY - Third Week - SATURDA

+ +

+ +

MENU (serves 2-4)

Budget Beef Roast, Au Jus
Pan-Roasted Potatoes
Herbed Green Peas and Celery

+ +

+ BUDGET BEEF ROAST +

Preparation time: none
Cooking time: see Chart and CHATTER, below

The budget cut of chuck beef is an excellent substitute for its elegant cousin, the Standing Rib Roast. It does not look the same, nor can it be carved the same way, being a chunk, or block, of meat. It's advantages are its lower price and lack of waste (no heavy bones and no outer layer of fat), plus its delicious flavor. It is basically a bit tougher than the usual roast beef, but proper cooking time should reduce it to a tender, succulent state. Follow the cooking charts and purchase suggestions below faithfully, and also be sure your oven temperature registers correctly. This is of prime importance for this or any roast and will assure several delicious meals.

HOW AND WHAT TO BUY:

1. Buy enough to last at least 2 meals with plenty of leftovers. It's poor economy to cook tiny roasts. For you, a 4- to 6-lb. one would be nice.
2. If the label reads, "First Block Chuck," "Standing Clod Roast," "Rump Roast," or just "Chuck Roast," it's what you want and what you can afford (79¢ per pound at this writing). If in doubt, ask the butcher. Show him this page!
3. All these cuts are sometimes sold "rolled" and "boneless." Then the price is higher, but they are easier to carve.

PREPARATION:

Two hours before cooking: Remove beef roast from refrigerator and place on rack in a roasting pan. This brings it gradually to room temperature. (If you sling it into the oven <u>cold</u>, straight from the refrigerator, add 15 minutes to the total cooking time, plus prayer.)

Turn the oven to 325. Close door. Let heat up for 10 minutes.

Then, place roast in oven on center rack, and time according to following <u>Beef Roast Chart</u>:

+ ROAST <u>WITH BONE</u> +	or	+ <u>BONELESS</u> ROLLED ROAST +
18-20 minutes per lb.	Rare	25-30 minutes per lb.
22-25 minutes per lb.	Medium	30-35 minutes per lb.
27-30 minutes per lb.	Well Done	35-40 minutes per lb.

<u>Example</u>: You have a 4- lb. roast with bone in. You want it done <u>very rare</u>. Multiply 18 minutes per lb. by 4 lb. That's 72 minutes, or 1 hour and 12 minutes roasting time in oven. Not bad!

+ <u>CHATTER</u> +

You would do well to let your roast sit for 10 minutes at back of stove once it is done. It will not cool off appreciably, and for some reason it's always easier to carve nicely after a short wait.

+ + + + + + + + + + + + + +

+ PAN-ROASTED POTATOES + Takes 1 hour

These potatoes, brown on the outside, tender inside, rely on the pan juices from the roast for their distinctive flavor. (If you do 6 potatoes today, you'll have 2 leftover for tomorrow.)

INGREDIENTS:

6 medium potatoes
1-2 teaspoons cooking oil (peanut or corn)

PREPARATION:

Peel potatoes. Cut in half, lengthwise. Rub them all over with cooking oil.
One hour before roast is done, put them on bottom of roasting pan. Let cook along with roast for 30 minutes. Then turn them over to brown other side. Cook 30 minutes more.
When done (fork-tender), remove potatoes, and roast, to a platter or carving board, and keep warm at back of stove while you whip up...

+ PAN GRAVY + Takes 3-4 minutes

This is the type referred to as au jus, meaning "with juice."

INGREDIENTS:

1/4 cup pan juices
2 cup hot water
2 beef bouillon cubes

Remove rack from roasting pan. Into nearby clean can or cup, pour off fat from pan slowly, leaving about 1/4 cup juices in the pan. (Save the can of fat!)
Put roasting pan on stove. Add 2 cups hot water and beef bouillon cubes. Turn heat to high. Let boil wildly 3 minutes, meanwhile scraping pan bottom with spoon to incorporate all collected meat and juices from pan. Remove from fire. This simple pan gravy is thin but delicious.

+ + + + + + + + + + + + + +

+ HERBED GREEN PEAS AND CELERY + Takes 10 minutes

INGREDIENTS:

2 stalks celery
1 package frozen peas
1/2 teaspoon basil or thyme
1 tablespoon butter or oil
1/4 teaspoon salt
Some pepper

Chop up 2 stalks celery in small dice.

Put peas, celery, and basil or thyme in saucepan. Add 1/2 cup water. Bring to boil. Separate frozen peas. Cover pan. Cook on low for 4-5 minutes.

Drain. Return peas to pan. Add 1 tablespoon butter or oil and salt and pepper. Mix. Cover till ready to serve.

\+ +

SUNDAY - Third Week - SUNDAY - Third Week - SUNDAY - Third Week - SUNDAY - Thir

\+ +

Most stores closed Sunday. Check refrigerator and staple shelf ahead for underlined ingredients.

\+ +

6 Suggestions for BEEF ROAST LEFTOVERS (serves 2)

BRUNCH:	1)	Roast Beef Hash 'n' Eggs
	2)	Steak 'n' Eggs with Onions
SUPPER:	3)	Simple Reheated-Beef Sandwiches
	4)	Beef Slices Barbecued
	5)	Wetback Stew
	6)	Hearty Beef Soup

\+ +

1) + ROAST BEEF HASH 'N' EGGS +

Chop 1 medium onion fine. Also, 1 clove of peeled garlic. Cut 2 slices (1/2"thick) of roast beef and dice up small as possible. Cut up 2 leftover potatoes as small as possible.

In large (12") skillet, melt 2-3 tablespoons butter or margarine over medium heat. Add onions and garlic. Cook over medium heat 3-4 minutes, till soft. Add chopped meat and potatoes. Stir to mix well. Cover skillet. Turn heat to low. Cook 20 minutes. Stir once or twice during cooking time.

Fry eggs in smaller skillet. When done, serve on top of hash.

\+ + + + + + + + + + + + + +

2) + STEAK 'N' EGGS WITH ONIONS +

Very British, this.

Peel and slice thin 1 large onion. Melt 2 tablespoons butter or margarine in small skillet over medium heat. Add onion. Cook gently 3-4 minutes.

While onion cooks, slice off 2 nice thick (at least 1/2") slices of rare beef. Drop them in skillet beside cooked onion. Fry on both sides 2-3 minutes.
Meanwhile, in second skillet, fry eggs. Serve "steaks" topped with onion and fried eggs.

+ + + + + + + + + + + + + +

3) + SIMPLE REHEATED-BEEF SANDWICHES +

Slice off some 1/2" thick beef slices.
Melt 1 tablespoon butter over medium heat. Add 1 tablespoon flour and stir a minutes. Remove from heat.
Gradually add 1 cup leftover pan gravy (or 1 cup hot water with 1 beef bouillon cube melted in it). Stir till smooth. Return to heat. Cook, stirring, till thickened (about 4-5 minutes).
Add beef slices to gravy in skillet. Let heat through (3-4 minutes).
Serve beef slices on bread or buttered toast, with gravy. Season with salt and pepper if necessary.

+ + + + + + + + + + + + + + +

4) + BEEF SLICES BARBECUED +

Cut off 3 or 4 slices beef 1/4" thick. Stack them and slice into 5-6 strips. Place in a greased or buttered skillet.
In mixing bowl, mix together: 3 tablespoons chili sauce, 1 tablespoon Worcestershire sauce, 1 1/2 teaspoon A-1 Sauce, 2-3 drops Tabasco (optional), and 1 peeled and smashed clove garlic.
Surround beef slices with mixture. Heat to boiling over high heat, then turn down to low and simmer 20 minutes, covered.
Leftover potatoes can be thickly slices right into the skillet and cooked with beef. Or, if potatoes vanished on Saturday, just boil up 3/4 cup Uncle Ben's converted rice in 1 1/2 cups of water for 20 minutes, and add that. Don't forget to turn down to simmer and to cover saucepan.
By the way, leftover potatoes can also be reheated, wrapped in foil, in a 350 oven for 20 minutes. Then peel, mash with fork, add butter, salt, and pepper.

+ + + + + + + + + + + + + + +

5) + WETBACK STEW + Preparation: 25 minutes in all

Peel and slice a large onion and a clove of garlic. Cut off 2-3 thick (1/2") slices beef, stack them, and slice into 5-6 strips. Slice 1-2 tomatoes, 1 green pepper, and any leftover potatoes. Open and drain 1 can kernel corn (not creamed variety).
Melt 3 tablespoons saved beef fat or bacon fat, or butter, in large (12") skillet over medium heat. Add onion and garlic. Cook 2-3 minutes.
Add tomatoes and green pepper. Cook 2-3 minutes more.

Add beef slices, stir, cover skillet. Cook 10 minutes.

Add corn and potatoes. Cover. Cook 4-5 minutes. Add 1/3 teaspoon salt and 1/4 teaspoon pepper. Stir well. Serve.

+ + + + + + + + + + + + + +

6) + HEARTY BEEF SOUP + Preparation: 15 minutes in all

In largest saucepan, melt 3 beef bouillon cubes in 3 cups hot water. (Add leftover pan gravy if you have any.) Add fistful of noodles.

Cut 2 thick (1/2") slices beef. Dice them. Also leftover potatoes. (A chopped onion and tomato are good in this, too.)

Bring pot to boil over high heat. Then turn to low, cover, and cook for 10 minutes.

If you have any leftover cooked vegetables (i.e., peas), add them to the pot now. Let simmer 1 minute. Serve with buttered toast.

+ + + + + + + + + + + + + +

MENUS for FOURTH WEEK

+ MONDAY +

Romeo's Chicken Cacciatore
Noodles
Jose's Salad

+ TUESDAY +

Chinese Steak
Chinese Fried Rice
Lindsay's Quick Russian-Dressing Salad

+ WEDNESDAY +

Meat Loaf
Short-Cut Mashed Potatoes
Church-Supper Cole Slaw

+ THURSDAY +

Old-Fashioned New England Boiled Dinner
Hot Rye Bread And Butter

+ FRIDAY +

Creamy Ham and Macaroni Casserole
A-Plus Salad

+ SATURDAY +

Roast Chicken
Giblet Gravy
Hasty Noodle Pudding
'Erbert's Herby String Beans

+ SUNDAY +

8 Suggestions for ROAST CHICKEN LEFTOVERS

+ Brunch: Scrambled Eggs with Chicken
Never-Fail Quick Creamed Chicken on toast

+ Supper: Reheated Chicken
Henny Penny's Spicy Chicken
Chinese Casserole
Chicken Scratch
Chicken Soup with Dumplings
Chicken Divan, Freestyle

+ +

Shopping - FOURTH WEEK - Shopping

+ +

BUY for MONDAY through SATURDAY (but, you should already have many of these items - so check before shopping):

+ Meats +

3-lb. chicken fryer, cut up
1 1/2-lb. boneless chuck steak, 1/2" thick
1 1/2-lb. ground chuck
1 1/2-lb. cottage ham
3 1/2- to 4 1/2-lb. roasting chicken

+ Canned Goods +

15-oz. can tomato sauce
4-oz. can mushroom pieces

+ Sundries +

1 pkg. wide noodles
1 pkg. Uncle Ben's converted rice
1 loaf frozen rye bread (optional)
1 pkg. elbow macaroni
1 pkg. narrow noodles
Cocktail sherry or Boone's Farm Apple Wine (optional)

+ Dairy Products +

Butter or margarine
Milk
Eggs
Shaker of grated Romano or Parmesan cheese
1/2 pint sour cream
1/2 pint cottage cheese

+ Vegetables +

4 medium onions
2 green peppers
Garlic
1 small head iceberg lettuce
1 avocado
1 small bunch scallions (green onions)
6 medium potatoes
1 small (1-lb.) cabbage
4 carrots (or 1 small bunch)
Celery
1 cucumber
1 Italian (red) onion (optional)
1 pkg. frozen string beans (or 1/2 lb. fresh)

+ STAPLES for FOURTH WEEK + Do you have:

Flour (unbleached or stone-ground if possible)
Salt
Pepper
Salad oil (peanut or corn)
Vinegar (wine or cider)
Chicken bouillon cubes
Bread
Bacon
Mayonnaise
Soy sauce (small bottle)
Ketchup
Chili sauce or barbecue sauce
Worcestershire sauce
Dry mustard
Regular mustard
Lemon juice (Real Lemon)
Instant minced onion (optional)
Garlic powder
Oregano
Thyme
Basil
Paprika

+ +

MENU (serves 2) — Romeo's Chicken Cacciatore
Noodles
Jose's Salad

+ +

+ ROMEO'S CHICKEN CACCIATORE +

Preparation: 15 minutes
Cooking: 1 hour

Two students at New York's International House contributed toward today's menu. You'll have to go far to find a better version of Romeo's Chicken, browned and simmered in a pungent, rich, red sauce: It's finito in 3 easy steps, and magnifico!

LINE UP YOUR INGREDIENTS:

3-lb. chicken fryer, cut up
2 tablespoons flour
1 teaspoon salt
1/2 teaspoon pepper
1/4 cup oil (peanut, corn)
2 medium onions
1 clove garlic
1 green pepper
1 can (15 oz.) tomato sauce
1 teaspoon oregano
1 teaspoon thyme
4-oz. can mushroom pieces

PREPARATION:

1. In paper bag, put flour, salt, and pepper. Wash chicken parts, dry well. Then shake in bag till each piece is well coated. In large (12") skillet, heat oil over medium heat. Add chicken pieces and brown 5 minutes on each side. Remove chicken to a platter or plate.
2. Peel and slice onions and garlic clove. Remove green pepper seeds. Slice pepper thinly. Add all these vegetables to oil left in skillet. Cook 2-3 minutes on medium heat. Stir a bit now and then.
3. Return chicken parts to skillet. Add: Tomato sauce, oregano, thyme, mushrooms with juice, salt and pepper. Cover. When sauce starts to bubble, turn to low heat and cover skillet. Simmer for 1 hour.

+ CHATTER +

There's a good gadget - a mesh skillet lid - to use when frying anything. Prevents grease from splattering into face and over stove top.

+ + + + + + + + + + + + + + +

+ NOODLES + Takes 10 minutes

INGREDIENTS:

4-oz. wide noodles
1 tablespoon butter or margarine
Salt

Bring 3 cups of water to a boil in saucepan over high heat. Add noodles. Cook at a boil uncovered for 8 minutes.

Drain into sieve. Return to saucepan. Add butter and salt. Mix. Cover to keep warm till dinner is ready.

+ + + + + + + + + + + + + +

+ JOSE'S SALAD +

A true South-of-the-border salad - simplicity itself and a crunchy delight. Mostly, you need to find a ripe (tender to the squeeze) avocado.

INGREDIENTS:

1/2 head iceberg lettuce
1 green pepper
1 ripe avocado

Slice lettuce fine into large mixing bowl. Remove green pepper seeds and slice pepper into bowl.

Peel off hard outer skin of avocado. Halve and remove pit. Slice into bowl with lettuce and green pepper.

+ DRESSING +

1 tablespoon vinegar (cider or wine)
3 tablespoons oil (peanut, corn)
1/2 teaspoon salt
1/4 teaspoon black pepper

Add all dressing ingredients to mixing bowl containing salad. Mix all well, 12-15 times. Refrigerate till chicken is ready.

+ CHATTER +

An avocado pit can be grown into a beautiful lush-looking houseplant.

+ + + + + + + + + + + + + +

+ +

MENU (serves 2) — Chinese Steak
Chinese Fried Rice
Lindsay's Quick Russian-Dressing Salad

+ +

+ CHINESE STEAK +

The cooking time for this is brief because you've taken the trouble to wait a bit beforehand while the meat has turned tender in its magic marinade.

LINE UP YOUR INGREDIENTS:

2-3 scallions (green onions)
1 clove garlic
2 tablespoons soy sauce
2 tablespoons sherry or Boone's Farm Apple Wine
1 1/2 lb. boneless chuck steak
2 tablespoons oil (peanut, corn)
1/2 cup chicken broth (1/2 chicken bouillon cube dissolved in 1/2 cup hot water)

PREPARATION:

Chop up scallions and garlic. Put on platter or pan large enough to hold the steak. Add soy sauce and sherry or wine. Stir all together.

Place steak on mixture. Let sit 15 minutes. Turn over and marinate other side 15 minutes more.

While steak marinates, melt 1/2 chicken bouillon cube in hot water. Put aside till later.

COOKING:

Heat large (12") iron skillet over high heat. Then, turn to medium heat.

Pour 1 tablespoon oil into skillet. Add steak. Cook 5 minutes.

Pour 2nd tablespoon oil into skillet and turn steak. Cook 5 minutes more.

Remove steak to large plate. Pour marinade into skillet with chicken broth. Cook quickly. Stir around for 1-2 minutes. Pour over steak. Serve.

+ CHATTER +

Whenever any alcoholic beverage is cooked, the alcohol content evaporates leaving only the flavor.

+ + + + + + + + + + + + + +

+ CHINESE FRIED RICE + 20 minutes

Fix this while steak is marinating.

If frozen or canned fried rice, follow package directions.
Otherwise (and cheaper), melt 1 tablespoon butter in saucepan. Add 3/4 cup Uncle Ben's converted rice. Stir around till browned.
Add 2 cups hot water and 2 chicken bouillon cubes. (If you have 2 stalks of celery and a carrot, chop them up and toss them in too.)
Bring to a boil. Cover. Turn to low heat. Cook 20 minutes, or till rice absorbs all liquid. Turn off heat. Leave covered to keep warm till steak's done.

+ + + + + + + + + + + + + +

+ LINDSAY'S QUICK RUSSIAN-DRESSING SALAD +

You can do this at the last minute, but it seems to pick up flavor if refrigerated a little while. Either way, it's easy and good.

INGREDIENTS:

1/2 small head iceberg lettuce
3 tablespoons mayonnaise
3 tablespoons ketchup

Into small mixing bowl, measure ketchup and mayonnaise. Mix well.
Cut lettuce half in half again, put on plates. Pour over lettuce wedges. Serve cold.

+ +
WEDNESDAY - Fourth Week - WEDNESDAY - Fourth Week - WEDNESDAY - Fourth Week - W
+ +

+ +

MENU (serves 2)

Meat Loaf
Short-Cut Mashed Potatoes
Church-Supper Cole Slaw

+ +

This meat loaf is highly recommended - made in larger quantity - as a budget party dish. Fast, cheap, and tastes good, especially for a batch of hungry male guests.

+ MEAT LOAF +

Preparation: 5-10 minutes
Baking: 1 hour

LINE UP YOUR INGREDIENTS:

1 1/2 lb. ground beef
3 tablespoons chili sauce
 or barbecue sauce
3 slices bread, torn up small
1 cup milk
1 egg

2 teaspoons salt
1/4 teaspoon pepper
1/4 teaspoon garlic powder
1 tablespoon Worcestershire sauce
1 tablespoon ketchup

PREPARATION:

Preheat oven to 350.
Championship time for mixing this is 3 minutes, if ingredients are lined up. Mix and bake it all in the same Pyrex ovenware bowl, or in a bread loaf pan. (Makes excellent sandwiches, too.)

Measure everything except first 2 ingredients into pan or bowl. Beat with a fork to mix well.

Add ground beef. Squish everything together with hands until well mixed. Pat down until smooth. Cover with chili sauce or barbecue sauce.

Bake at 350 for 1 hour. Remove from oven. Pour off excess fat before serving.

+ CHATTER +

Next time, put 2 shelled hard-boiled eggs inside center of meat loaf before baking. A surprise when sliced and adds a nice flavor.

+ + + + + + + + + + + + + +

+ SHORT-CUT MASHED POTATOES +

About 1 hour

If you have no proper potato masher, or you just can't face the job, this method will get you there. BUT, start these before you get going on Meat Loaf.

INGREDIENTS:

2-4 medium potatoes
3 tablespoons butter or margarine

1/4 cup milk (or more)
Salt and pepper

PREPARATION:

Preheat oven to 350.

Scrub potatoes clean and dry them. (If you can eat 2 each, use 4.)

Place on center rack of oven. Now mix Meat Loaf and put in oven. When potatoes have cooked about 1 hour, feel them. If soft when pinched or pressed with fingers, they're done.

Cut potatoes open. Scoop out insides onto plate. Add butter, milk, and 1/2 teaspoon salt. Mash well with back of fork. (You will need extra butter, milk, and salt if you've used 4 potatoes.) Add a couple of dashes of pepper, mash and mix. Serve.

+ CHATTER +

Don't forget that potato skins, or shells, are wonderful spread inside with butter and eaten folded over like a sandwich. Besides, the skins contain large amounts of vitamin C and iron. Consider that as you start to dump them - and reconsider.

\+ + + + + + + + + + + + + +

+ CHURCH-SUPPER COLE SLAW + Preparation: 10 minutes

This is another salad that improves with "sitting time" in the refrigerator. But, it can be served immediately, too. Whichever...you can't hurt it. It's always delicious.

LINE UP YOUR INGREDIENTS:

1/2 head small (1-lb.) cabbage
1 large carrot
4-5 heaping tablespoons mayonnaise
1 teaspoon vinegar
3 teaspoons oil (peanut, corn)
1/4 teaspoon salt
1/4 teaspoon pepper

PREPARATION:

Cut cabbage half in half again, and remove the hard heart. Now slice cabbage leaves as thin as possible. Place in medium mixing bowl. Grate carrot, or chop fine, and add.

Add all other ingredients in order given. Mix thoroughly. Taste and correct seasoning if more salt is needed.

\+ + + + + + + + + + + + + +

Never shop when you're hungry.

+ +

+ +

MENU (serves 2) — Old-Fashioned New England Boiled Dinner
Hot Rye Bread and Butter

+ +

+ OLD-FASHIONED NEW ENGLAND BOILED DINNER +

Preparation: 4 minutes
Takes 1 1/2 hours in all

This whole dinner is always cooked in the same pot. The ham-flavored water gives ordinary potatoes and cabbage a superb new taste.

LINE UP YOUR INGREDIENTS:

1 1/2-lb. cottage ham
2 medium potatoes
1/2 head cabbage (1/2 lb.)
2 fat carrots (optional)

PREPARATION:

Ham: Take ham out of all wrappings, place in large saucepan, cover with water. Bring to boil, then lower heat, cover pan, simmer for 1 1/4 hours (or according to package directions). Remove to plate.

Potatoes: Peel, cut into thick 1" slices. Add them to the ham pot for its last 20 minutes of cooking time. Test potatoes for doneness with a fork. They should pierce easily but should not be mushy. When done, remove potatoes to a warm plate. Cover them with a paper towel or clean cloth while the cabbage is cooking. (The towel will absorb excess moisture, making the potatoes deliciously dry and mealy, instead of watery.)

Carrots: Scrub, quarter, and add at same time as potatoes. Take out at same time.

Cabbage: Rinse under cold water. Peel off outer leaf or two if wilted. Cut into about 4 big wedges. Have it ready to pop into water when ham, potatoes, and carrots removed. Turn heat up to medium or more. Cook cabbage, covered, for 10 to 15 minutes or until the hard white center core can pierced with a fork. It should be tender but not falling apart.

To serve: Serve slices of ham with wedges of cabbage, potato slices, carrots. Have cold butter handy to be eaten with each bite of potato.

+ CHATTER +

1. To select a good cottage ham, squeeze it gently all over. The one which feels firmest contains most lean meat, least fat.

2. If your market has it, a loaf of frozen rye bread is terrific heated up in the oven and served with lots of butter. Follow package directions. Usually takes 45 minutes for frozen loaf, 20 minutes for thawed. Slice and serve piping hot.

+ +

MENU (serves 2) — Creamy Ham and Macaroni Casserole
A-Plus Salad

+ +

+ CREAMY HAM AND MACARONI CASSEROLE +

Preparation: 15 minutes
Cooking: 30-40 minutes

A small amount of leftover ham is combined with macaroni and a highly seasoned cream sauce to stretch to a full meal.

LINE UP YOUR INGREDIENTS:

1 1/2 cups elbow macaroni
1 to 2 cups leftover cottage ham, cut up
2 tablespoons oil
1 1/2 tablespoons flour
1 cup milk
1/2 teaspoon dry mustard
1/2 teaspoon regular mustard
1/4 teaspoon garlic powder
1/2 teaspoon salt
1/4 cup grated cheese (Romano or Parmesan)

PREPARATION:

Preheat oven to 350.

Macaroni: In large saucepan, boil macaroni in 3 cups water for 8 minutes until just tender. Drain in sieve and rinse under cold water. Let stand until ready to use.

Ham: Cut leftover ham in 1/2" slices. Cut these into 1" squares, removing most (but not all) of the fat. Place ham in ovenproof casserole.

Cream Sauce: In small skillet, heat cooking oil over medium heat. When hot, add flour, stirring constantly to prevent lumps. Allow this to cook for 2 or 3 minutes until the flour is cooked. Gradually add milk, stirring constantly to smooth lumps. (A wire whisk helps.) When smooth and creamy, add the 2 mustards and the garlic powder and salt.

Pour cream sauce over ham in the casserole. Add the grated cheese and toss all to mix very well. Cover casserole and place in 350 oven until good and hot, 30-40 minutes.

+ + + + + + + + + + + + + + +

+ A-PLUS SALAD +

10 minutes

Do this while the casserole is baking. All you need is a love of raw vegetables, a sharp chopping knife, and a wood surface to cut on.

INGREDIENTS:

1 green pepper
1 carrot
2 stalks celery
1 medium cucumber
1 medium Italian (red) onion (optional)

1 teaspoon lemon juice
3 tablespoons peanut oil (or corn)
1/2 teaspoon water
1/4 teaspoon basil
1/4 teaspoon salt

Remove seeds from green pepper. Slice. Chop up. Put in large bowl.

Wash, but do <u>not</u> peel, carrot. Cut off stem end. Slice and chop. Add to mixing bowl.

Chop up celery, leaves and all. Add to bowl. Peel, slice and chop up cucumber. Add to bowl. Peel, slice, and chop Italian onion. Add to bowl.

In small separate bowl or cup, mix all ingredients for dressing. Stir together vigorously. Pour over raw salad vegetables. Mix. Refrigerate till dinner is ready.

+ +

SATURDAY - Fourth Week - SATURDAY - Fourth Week - SATURDAY - Fourth Week - SATU

+ +

+ +

MENU (serves 2)

Roast Chicken
Giblet Gravy
Hasty Noodle Pudding
'Erbert's Herby String Beans

+ +

+ <u>ROAST CHICKEN</u> +

Preparation: 5 minutes
Cooking: 2 hours,
or see CHART below

A roast chicken, like any other roasted meat, is simple to prepare, needing only the temperature chart below and a steady oven. High in protein, low in calories and cost, roast chicken is a one-pan, no-watch operation, and serves 2 for two meals - see 8 possibilities to pick from tomorrow, Sunday.

LINE UP YOUR INGREDIENTS:

3 1/2- to 4 1/2-lb. roasting chicken
1 teaspoon salt
Some pepper
Some paprika

Pieces of chicken fat
(or 1 strip of bacon, or
2 tablespoons butter)

PREPARATION:

Turn oven to 325.

Remove chicken giblets (neck, liver, heart, gizzard) and set aside. Cut away any extra fat inside bird, near neck or tail, and save it.

Wash chicken under cold tap water quickly, inside and out. Pat dry. Salt and pepper inside and out. (Put 1/2 teaspoon salt in hand and rub it inside. Dust with paprika if you have some around.

Place chicken on roasting-pan rack on its back (breast up, legs in air).

If you found extra pieces of chicken fat inside the bird, lay them on the breast and upper thighs. If not, lay on a strip of bacon, or smear butter over breast.

Place roasting pan on center rack in oven. Roast for 2-2 1/2 hours. To test for doneness: After 2 hours, pierce leg with tines of fork. If clear, not pinkish, juice runs out, it's ready.

+ CHICKEN ROASTING CHART +

Type	Weight	Hours	Oven Temperature
Broiler/Fryer	1 1/2 to 3 lbs.	1 to 1 1/2	375
Roaster	3 1/2 to 6 lbs	2 to 3	325
Capon	5 to 7 lbs	2 1/2 to 3 1/2	325

+ GIBLET GRAVY +

Preparation: 10 minutes
Cooking: 2 hours

Start this as soon as roast chicken goes into oven.

INGREDIENTS:

Chicken giblets (neck, heart, and gizzard)
3 chicken bouillon cubes (or 1 teaspoon salt)
4 cups water
1 teaspoon instant minced onion (optional)
2 tablespoons pan juices
2 tablespoons flour

Put giblets in sauce pan (don't use liver). Add bouillon cubes, water, onion. Bring to boil over high heat. Turn heat to low. Cover saucepan. Simmer 2 hours.

When roast chicken is done, remove from pan to platter. Pour off pan juices ("drippings"), BUT leave at least 2 tablespoons in roasting pan. At stove, over medium heat, add flour to roasting pan. Stir a minute.

Now, slowly, add giblet "stock" from saucepan, stirring all the time. When all the stock is in the pan and smoothly mixed, turn heat to low and simmer 3-4 minutes.

Cut up the giblet meat into small dice and put them in gravy. Taste and add salt if necessary, but if you've used chicken bouillon cubes, it probably won't be.

+ CHICKEN CHATTER +

1. To understand your market's various labels: A "broiler/fryer" chicken can be broiled, fried, or roasted. By correct poultry standards they are 9 weeks old and weigh 1 1/2-3 1/2 lb. A labeled "roaster" chicken is 12 weeks old, and therefore heavier, 3 1/2-6 lb. (useful when you plan to get more meals from one effort). A "hen," "stewing hen," "fowl," or "bro-hen," is older (1 1/2 years) and tougher, and is mainly used for boiling (to make soups, salads, etc.). "Capon" is an altered rooster, weighs 5-7 lb., is delicious roasted, and is much more expensive.

2. Some people put the chicken liver into the gravy, cut up finely, to simmer the last few minutes. Others save it to fry with eggs for breakfast. In any case, since liver is THE most nutritionally important meat you can get, you certainly should make sure to eat it sometime, and soon.

+ + + + + + + + + + + + + +

+ HASTY NOODLE PUDDING +

Preparation: 10 minutes
Cooking: 30 minutes

This casserole is great with chicken, pork, veal, or ham. For a party it can be doubled or tripled, made hours ahead, and baked shortly before serving.

LINE UP YOUR INGREDIENTS:

2 cups (6 oz.) narrow noodles
1 small clove garlic
Some oil
3/4 cup sour cream
1/2 cup cottage cheese
2 teaspoons Worcestershire sauce
1 teaspoon butter or margarine

PREPARATION:

Preheat oven to 325. (If pudding bakes with roast chicken, your oven is already preheated)

Boil noodles in 6 cups water till tender, about 7-8 minutes.

Chop up garlic clove very fine (or use 1/4 teaspoon garlic powder).

With some oil, lightly grease inside of small casserole (or small iron skillet, or a bread loaf pan).

Drain noodles at sink in sieve. Put them in greased casserole. Add all other ingredients except butter. Stir a minute, mixing all well. Dot top with bits of butter.

Cover casserole, or lacking a cover, improvise with aluminum foil. Place in 325 oven, on upper rack, for 30 minutes. Remove from oven. Keep covered till dinner is ready.

+ 'ERBERT'S HERBY STRING BEANS + 10 minutes

INGREDIENTS:

1 package frozen string beans (or 1/2 lb. fresh)
1 small onion
1/2 teaspoon thyme
1/4 teaspoon salt
1 tablespoon butter or margarine

Peel, slice, and chop up onion. Put it in a saucepan. Add string beans, thyme, salt, and 1/2 cup water.

Bring to boil over high heat. Separate beans. Then cover, turn heat to low, and simmer according to directions on box. (Fresh Beans require about 1 cup water and cook, covered, for 8 minutes.) Drain (save juice for soup). Return to pan. Add butter and serve.

+ +

SUNDAY - Fourth Week - SUNDAY - Fourth Week - SUNDAY - Fourth Week - SUNDAY - F

+ +

Have you checked refrigerator and staple shelf for underlined ingredients? It's Sunday, stores are closed.

+ +

8 Suggestions for ROAST CHICKEN LEFTOVERS (serves 2)

BRUNCH:

1) Scrambled Eggs with Chicken
2) Never-Fail Quick Creamed Chicken on Toast
3) Reheated Chicken
4) Henny Penny's Spicy Chicken
5) Chinese Casserole
6) Chicken Scratch
7) Chicken Soup with Dumplings
8) Chicken Divan, Freestyle

+ +

1) + SCRAMBLED EGGS WITH CHICKEN +

Slice and chop up 1 medium-size onion. Slice off 2 generous slices of chicken; cut into bite-size pieces.

Use large iron skillet. Melt 2 tablespoons butter (or oil). Add onion, cook over medium heat 2-3 minutes, or till onion is limp. Add chicken. Cook 1-2 minutes more.

Crack 2-3 eggs per person into skillet. Stir quickly and add 1/4 teaspoon salt, 1/4 teaspoon pepper, and 1/4 teaspoon garlic powder (optional). Keep stirring till eggs are set to your favorite consistancy. This is very good served with thick slices of tomatoes and hot buttered toast.

\+ + + + + + + + + + + + + + +

2) + NEVER-FAIL QUICK CREAMED CHICKEN ON TOAST + 10 minutes

Slice off and cut up 3 thick pieces of chicken.

In iron skillet melt 3 tablespoons butter over medium heat. Add 3 tablespoons flour. Stir 1 minute. Slowly, add 2 cups milk, stirring all the time so you don't get lumps. When blended, add 2 chicken bouillon cubes, mashing them with back of spoon to make them dissolve faster. Let mixture bubble and thicken, stirring now and then, for about 5-8 minutes.

Add chicken. Cook 2-3 minutes more, stirring some. Serve over buttered toast (2 slices per person). Tastes good with a few sliced olives on top, or some chopped parsley. Anyway, taste and add a little salt and pepper if necessary.

\+ + + + + + + + + + + + + + +

As you've now discovered from the past 3 Sundays, leftovers require a fondness for combining bits and pieces lurking uneaten in the refrigerator. You must also have a fair knowledge of how to reheat. These concluding 5 recipes prove the thesis: Improvisation is the secret of successful leftovers.

3) + REHEATED CHICKEN + 15-20 minutes in all

You simply slice off all the chicken you think you'll want for supper. Use a small skillet. Pour in at least 1 cup gravy. Warm it on a medium heat for 3-4 minutes. Add chicken slices. Warm 2-3 minutes. If you want to serve it on toast, make the toast while the chicken warms through. Butter it. It's better buttered.

By the way: If there's no gravy around, wrap chicken slices in foil, put in a 350 oven for 15-20 minutes. And, reheat any leftover Hasty Noodle Pudding, covered in the same oven for the same length of time.

\+ + + + + + + + + + + + + + +

4) + HENNY PENNY'S SPICY CHICKEN + Preparation: 10 minutes
Cooking: 15-20 minutes

When you feel the sky is falling, financially or otherwise, try this cheap recipe and be a foxy-loxy. (Ugh!)

Slice off 3-4 pieces of chicken. Cut in bite-size chunks. Slice, and chop

1 onion, 1 green pepper (remove seeds first), 2 stalks of celery. Fry 2 slices regular bacon in large skillet. Remove bacon and drain on paper towel or newspaper. Crumble bacon. Leave bacon fat in skillet.

Heat on medium, add to skillet onion, green pepper, and celery. Cook 4-5 minutes, till onion is transparent. Sprinkle in 1 tablespoon flour and 1 teaspoon curry powder. Stir 1 minute. Remove from heat. Add 2 cups leftover gravy (or 2 cups hot water plus 2 chicken bouillon cubes).

Turn heat to low. Simmer, covered, 10 minutes. Add crumbled bacon. Serve on toast or over noodles. (Noodles: Boil 1 cup noodles in 3 cups water for 8 minutes, and drain.)

+ + + + + + + + + + + + + + +

5) + CHINESE CASSEROLE +

Preparation: 5 minutes
Cooking: 30 minutes

Buy ahead for this one.

Grease a casserole or an iron skillet (12"). Open and drain: 1 can bean sprouts, 1 small jar sliced pimentos, 1 smallest can peas (save juice!). Put all in casserole. Add 3 thick slices chicken, cut in finger lengths. Add 1 can cream of celery soup and 1 can french-fried onions. Stir all together. Cover.

Bake in 350 oven for 30 minutes. Serve on plain white rice. (Rice: Simmer 1 cup of Uncle Ben's converted rice in 2 1/2 cups boiling water for 20 minutes, covered, on low heat.

+ + + + + + + + + + + + + + +

6) + CHICKEN SCRATCH +

10 minutes

A cold summer supper: Salad, anyone? Get a large mixing bowl. Slice off 3 large portions of chicken. Cut up into bite-size pieces. Slice and chop up whatever you have, any (or all, or at least 2) of the following: 1 green pepper, 1 very small onion, 2-3 stalks celery, leftover string beans, an apple, 2 medium carrots. Add 3 generous tablespoons mayonnaise and 1/2 teaspoon lemon juice. Mix and stir well. Serve on lettuce leaves, or tear up lettuce and mix right into salad.

+ + + + + + + + + + + + + + +

7) + CHICKEN SOUP WITH DUMPLINGS +

Cooking: 1 1/2-2 hours

Remove all chicken from bones and carcass. Cut up meat in dice. Put in refrigerator. Place bones, skins, etc., in largest saucepan. Add 6 cups water plus 1 teaspoon salt. Add a cut-up onion plus 3 stalks celery and leaves, cut up. Bring to boil over high heat. Turn to low. Cover. Simmer for 1 1/2 hours.

Strain broth through sieve into mixing bowl. Discard bones and vegetables. Return soup to pot. Add cut-up chicken.

DUMPLINGS: Beat 1 egg in a largish mixing bowl. Add 1 teaspoon salt, 1/2 cup milk, 1 1/2 cups flour. Stir till smooth.

Now bring soup to a boil over high heat. Drip or push dumpling batter by tablespoons into boiling soup. Cover. Cook 10 minutes. Remove a test dumpling spoon. Pull apart with 2 forks. If dry and not gummy inside, dumplings are done. If dampish, continue cooking in covered pot 5 minutes more.

+ + + + + + + + + + + + + + +

8) + CHICKEN DIVAN, FREESTYLE + Preparation: 5 minutes
Cooking: 1/2 hour

Gourmet restaurants charge plenty for something very close to this concoction. Shop ahead for it.

Thaw 1 box frozen broccoli bits and lay them in the bottom of a greased, medium-size oven casserole. Add about 1 cup bite-size chicken pieces (or more if you have it - white meat is preferred).

In a separate bowl, mix 1 pkg. dried chicken noodle soup mix, 1/2 cup or more seasoned bread crumbs, 1 small (8-oz.) carton sour cream, and 1 cup water. Pour this mixture over the chicken and broccoli. Dust top with grated Romano or Parmesan cheese.

Bake uncovered in 350 oven 1/2 hour, or until sauce is bubbling. Important: 5 minutes before serving, stir casserole contents gently but thoroughly to redistribute flavors.

+ + + + + + + + + + + + + + +

+ +

We figure it could have taken you a whole term to get through these four weeks of menus and recipes. By now, you must be some sort of local celebrity. . . that character who knows how to SURVIVE in a kitchen! People must be saying - well, see next page for what they're saying . . .

+ +

BOY!

Can you cook!

PARTY MENUS

+ PARTY #1 +

Ham, Baked or Boiled
Tamale Pie San Diego U.
Tossed Green Salad

+ PARTY #2 +

Parker's Steak Sandwiches
Baked Beans
Creamy Vegetable Salad

+ PARTY #3 +

Jo's Sloppy Joes
All-American Potato Salad

+ PARTY #4 +

Skeet's Hot-Dog Salad
Crusty Bread

+ PARTY #5 +

Shish Kebab
Kasha (Buckwheat Groats)
Slavic Potato Salad

+ PARTY #6 +

Very-Little-Coin Masterpiece
Caesar Salad

+ PARTY #7 +

Jack's Best Stew
Hard Rolls or Crusty Bread
Tossed Green Salad

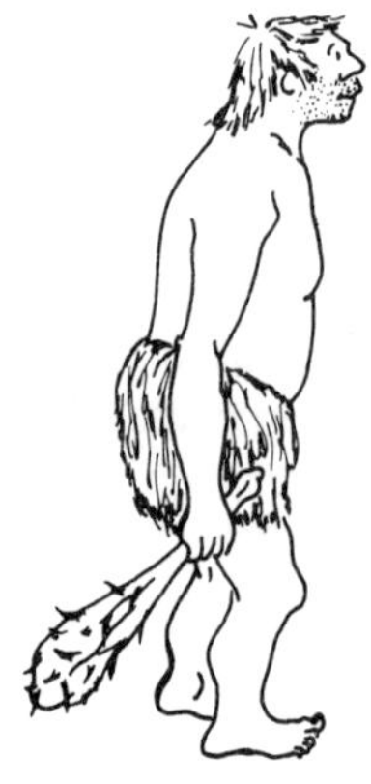

+ +

PARTIES - PARTIES - PARTIES

+ +

A PARTY can be thrown together in a half hour while guests are there, or it can be prepared completely in advance. Your personality decides which style is yours. This chapter has fast and slow dinners, some cheap, some costly, plus appetizer dips. Some DRINKS and DESSERTS are in next chapters. Do make dessert ahead if you add one to your menu.

+ +

These recipes, too, (find them in the Index) make fine party fare:

McCrystle's Survival Casserole
Don't Clam Up Spaghetti
Meat Loaf (make in largest skillet)
Roast Chicken
Sean's Fiji Chicken Casserole
Spaghetti with Meat Sauce
Spaghetti Mysterioso
Jon's Chicken Spare Ribs (make good appetizers)
Sean's Roast Rhinoceros

+ +

+ CALMING HINTS +

In multiplying a recipe to feed more people, salt and herb flavors can become too strong. Do not increase them in direct proportion; use a little less than that. You can always add more, to taste, before serving.

It's also a good idea to do all the multiplication for amounts of ingredients in advance. Write it down. You can lose track of what you're doing if you try to figure and cook simultaneously.

REMEMBER to CHECK ALL INGREDIENTS in RECIPES and make a COMPLETE MARKET LIST!

+ +

+ 4 SNACKING GOOD DIPS +

The best thing to appease ravenous friends while the pot bubbles is - food. Dips are the time-honored solution. The first three here are quick whip-ups, the fourth takes advance preparation. All are excellent.

+ WEST COAST ONION DIP +

In a bowl, mix 1 package of Lipton's dried onion soup mix with 1 pint of sour cream. Stir well. Refrigerate till needed. Potato or corn chips dip fine into this. Raw vegetables cut into sticks are even better.

+ EAST COAST CLAM DIP +

Chop a small onion very fine. Open and drain 1 small can of minced clams. Put onion and clams in a mixing bowl with 1/2 pint sour cream. Mix well. Refrigerate till needed. Suggest potato chips or raw vegetables here, again.

+ + + + + + + + + + + + + + +

+ ROYAL CAVIAR DIP +

Try it . . . You'll like it.

In mixing bowl, mix 1 small (2-oz.) jar lumpfish (black) caviar with 1 pint sour cream. Mix very well, till grayish. Not so pretty, but it's good. A great dipper with this is celery stalks - also raw zucchini cut in finger lengths (wash first, but don't peel).

+ + + + + + + + + + + + + + +

+ GUACAMOLE +

Here it is! Peel 1 large ripe avocado. It must be soft to the touch, but not mushy. Mash it in a bowl with a fork. (Save the pit.)

Grate a small (golf-ball size) onion. Add to avocado.

Put a ripe tomato in boiling water 2 minutes. Peel it. Chop it fine.

Add tomato, 1/2 tablespoon vinegar, and 1/2 teaspoon salt to avocado. Mix all well. Bury pit in the middle. Refrigerate. Before serving, remove pit. (Its presence keeps mixture green.) Fritos are perfect for dipping into this.

+ CHATTER +

Avocados (or Calavos) done this way and served on lettuce make a fine salad. Guacamole is a must with meals in Mexico.

+ + + + + + + + + + + + + + +

+ +

MENU (serves 6-8)

Tamale Pie San Diego U.
Boiled Ham
Tossed Green Salad

+ +

+ TAMALE PIE SAN DIEGO U. +

Preparation: 15 minutes
Cooking: 1 hour
Waiting: 45 minutes

This casserole-type recipe can also be made and served in a skillet or roasting pan. A firm thick pudding, it is redolent with mouth-watering flavors of corn, cheese, and Mexican seasonings. Although it has a special affinity with ham, it can be equally successful served with chicken or turkey. Please note its "waiting time" above. This is absolutely necessary in the firming up process. Otherwise, you have soup!

LINE UP YOUR INGREDIENTS:

2 cans or jars tamales (13-oz. size)
2 medium cans creamed corn (1 lb.)
1 medium can pitted black olives
4 tablespoons butter (1/2 stick)
1 small can tomato sauce (8 oz.)
1 cup yellow corn meal
1/2 lb. American cheese

PREPARATION:

Preheat oven to 350.

Open all cans and jars. Drain off olive juice. Cut olives in half. Grate American cheese on grater's largest holes, or chop in small pieces.

Using 9" x 13" roasting pan or largest (12") iron skillet, melt butter over medium heat at stove. Remove pan to counter. Add American cheese, corn, halved olives, tomato sauce, cornmeal.

Wash hands. Now dump in tamales and all juices. Remove husks (or wrappings). With fingers, break tamales into small pieces. Stir all together till well mixed. Place pie on middle oven rack, uncovered, for 1 hour.

Remove to fireproof surface. Pie will be a bit runny; allow to cool (and harden) 45 minutes or more. Fifteen minutes before serving, return to 350 oven to warm through. (Serves 6-8.)

+ + + + + + + + + + + + + + +

+ BOILED HAM +

A cottage ham or ham butt is a particularly juicy variety that's easy to prepare for a group. It usually comes in a plastic or see-through wrapping which you remove. Figure on 1/2 lb. per person. Put in boiling water, turn to medium heat, and cook 30 minutes per pound. (If you are serving 8 or more, you may need to buy 2 little hams. But, cook as one! Don't add to the cooking time.) Serve on platter or plate, and slice.

+ + + + + + + + + + + + + + +

+ TOSSED GREEN SALAD +

Do this ahead or while Tamale Pie is hardening. Wash, dry, and tear into bite-size pieces a large head of romaine or Boston lettuce. Refrigerate. When ham and pie are ready, pour French Dressing (page 41) on salad in bowl, toss 15 times, and serve.

+ + + + + + + + + + + + + + +

+ CHATTER +

1. Tamale Pie can be made earlier in day or the day before, and reheated.
2. Tamale Pie can be reheated over and over, either in same pan in 300 oven for 20 minutes, or over low heat on stove for 10 minutes.
3. When purchasing cottage ham or ham butt, try to buy a solid-feeling one for more meat content, less fat. Squeeze a few.

+ +

PARTY #2 - PARTY #2 - PARTY #2 - PARTY #2 - PARTY #2 - PARTY #2 - PARTY #2 - PA

+ +

+ +

MENU (serves 8) — Parker's Steak Sandwiches
Baked Beans
Creamy Vegetable Salad

+ +

Timing:
Steak - Marinates 6 to 8 hours
Broils 12 minutes
Beans - Preparation: 10 minutes
Baking: 1 1/2 to 2 hours
Salad - Preparation: 5 minutes
Refrigerate if possible

+ +

No last-minute hassle to this menu. Both the baked beans and salad may be prepared in advance. The steak is sliced thin, served in hot dog buns so it will feed twice as many people. Because it has been marinating all day in a powerful sauce, it should require no further seasoning and needs only to be broiled and sliced after guests have arrived.

+ PARKER'S STEAK SANDWICHES +

16 hot dog buns
1 1/2" thick boneless round steak (about 3 lb.)

Pierce steak all over with a fork; make deep holes every half inch or so. Place it in a long roasting pan. Pour over it the following marinade:

+ MARINADE +

LINE UP YOUR INGREDIENTS and mix in a bowl:

2 tablespoons meat tenderizer
1 tablespoon chopped onion, or 2 teaspoons instant minced onion
2 teaspoons thyme
1 tablespoon oregano
1 bay leaf
1 cup vinegar (cider or wine)
1/2 cup oil (corn or peanut)
3 tablespoons lemon juice
1/2 teaspoon pepper

Cover pan with plastic or foil. Let steak sit in marinade at room temperature 6 to 8 hours. Turn it over now and then.

To broil: Pour marinade out of pan. Save.

Place steak on rack in roasting pan. Broil 7" from flame, about 8 minutes on each side. It should be pink, not blood rare. Remove steak to a cutting board or warm serving platter. Let it rest for 10 minutes to make it easier to carve.

Slice it paper thin, and, before placing in buns, dip each slice in leftover marinade. Use 2 or 3 thin slices per bun. (Serves 8.)

+ CHATTER +

Buns taste better if toasted under the broiler about 20 seconds.

+ + + + + + + + + + + + + +

+ BAKED BEANS +

Preparation: 5 minutes
Baking: 1 1/2 to 2 hours

LINE UP YOUR INGREDIENTS:

2 large cans pork and beans (4 lb.) such as Campbell's
1 medium onion, chopped
1/2 to 3/4 cup dark brown sugar
2 cups ketchup
4 strips bacon, cut in small pieces

Preheat oven to 350.

This is not a scientific formula. Just mix the first 4 ingredients well in a casserole. Taste to see if you want more sugar or ketchup. (Remember that flavors will concentrate as the beans cook.) Top with the bacon pieces. Bake, uncovered, in 350 oven, 1 1/2 to 2 hours, or until a crust forms. (Serves 8.)

+ + + + + + + + + + + + + + +

+ CREAMY VEGETABLE SALAD +

An ancient French recipe in modern dress, this salad is a double-duty dish - your vegetables and salad in one. Refrigerate ahead. The colder the better.

LINE UP YOUR INGREDIENTS:

Two 1-lb. cans mixed vegetables
3 teaspoons lemon juice
1/2 teaspoon basil
4-5 tablespoons mayonnaise
Large lettuce leaves (optional)
Salt
Pepper

Open cans of mixed vegetables. Drain them into your soup pot (or drink juice, or save it to make good gravy sometime).

In mixing bowl: Measure lemon juice, basil, mayonnaise. Mix well. Add vegetables. Stir gently till vegetables are well-coated. Taste for flavor. About 1/2 teaspoon salt and a couple of good dashes of pepper should do it. If not, try a bit more salt. Stir again and refrigerate till dinner is ready.

You can serve this on lettuce leaf, or just plain plopped on dinner plates. Good both ways, of course. (Serves 8.)

+ +

PARTY #3 - PARTY #3 - PARTY #3 - PARTY #3 - PARTY #3 - PARTY #3 - PARTY #3 - PA

+ +

+ +

MENU (serves 6-8)
Jo's Sloppy Joes
All-American Potato Salad

+ +

+ JO'S SLOPPY JOES +

Preparation: 10 minutes
Cooking: 15 minutes

This is the fastest, cheapest get-together menu on record, and if you've kept your staples shelf up-to-date, all you need to buy is the hamburger meat, buns, and tomato paste.

INGREDIENTS:

2 lb. ground beef (or hamburger)
8-12 hamburger buns
1 small (6-oz.) can tomato paste
1 1/4 cups water
1/2 teaspoon salt
1 tablespoon instant minced onion
1/4 teaspoon garlic powder,
(or, 1 clove garlic, chopped)
1/2 teaspoon thyme
1/2 teaspoon oregano
1/4 teaspoon sugar

PREPARATION:

In large (12") skillet, brown hamburger meat for 2-3 minutes over medium heat.

Add all ingredients in order given. Stir. Bring to a bubble over high heat. Turn to low. Cover. Simmer for 15 minutes. Meanwhile:

Turn oven to 350: Slice buns in half. Put them on rack in oven to heat, 10 minutes. Remove buns. Place a generous splash (2-3 tablespoons) of the Sloppy Joe mixture on each bun, and serve. Squishy, but delicious. (Serves 6-8.)

\+ + + + + + + + + + + + + +

\+ ALL-AMERICAN POTATO SALAD +

In the morning (or several hours ahead): Boil 5 potatoes 20-30 minutes. Boil 2 eggs 20 minutes. When potatoes are fork tender, they're done. Refrigerate potatoes and eggs till 1 or 2 hours before dinner.

INGREDIENTS:

1 sour pickle (about 3" long)
1 small (3 1/2-oz.) jar pimientos
5 heaping tablespoons mayonnaise
1 teaspoon mild mustard
1/2 teaspoon salt
1/4 teaspoon sugar

PREPARATION:

Peel cold boiled potatoes. Cut in bite-size chunks. Place in large bowl. Shell cold hard-boiled eggs. Slice. Add to potatoes in bowl. Chop pickle. Also, drain and chop pimientos. Add to bowl.

In a small bowl: Add all other ingredients. Stir well to mix. Add to potato-salad bowl. Stir again till well mixed. Refrigerate till dinner. Taste for more salt. Serve.

This is sometimes served on a bed of lettuce leaves. That's not a must, just pretty. It's just as good straight out of the bowl. (Serves 6-8.)

\+ + + + + + + + + + + + + +

+ +

MENU (serves 6) — Skeet's Hot-Dog Salad
Crusty Bread

+ +

+ SKEET'S HOT DOG SALAD +

Total time: 30 minutes

Served fresh from the skillet, this is fun to make while people are watching. The mixture of textures and temperatures (soft hot potatoes, crisp cold cucumbers, etc., firm hot frankfurters) is quite surprising. Serve with it a long loaf of crusty French bread (warm it in the oven and put it right on the table so guests can tear off chunks). The meal is complete.

LINE UP YOUR INGREDIENTS:

6 medium potatoes
6 slices bacon
6-8 skinless frankfurters
1/2 head romaine lettuce, in pieces
1 cucumber, peeled, sliced
2 small onions, peeled, sliced
2 stalks celery, sliced
1 1/3 tablespoon flour
1 tablespoon sugar
1 3/4 teaspoon salt
Dashes of pepper
1 cup water
1/3 cup vinegar (5 tablespoons + 1 teaspoon)

The potatoes and bacon can cook while you prepare other ingredients. Potatoes: Wash, do not pare. Cover with water in a saucepan. Boil about 30 minutes or until fork tender. Bacon: Fry until crisp in large (12") skillet. Drain on paper towel.

Meanwhile: Wash romaine lettuce, break into bite-size pieces. Pare cucumber, slice thin. Peel onions, slice thin. Break slices into rings. Wash celery, slice into 1/2" pieces.

Heat franks in with boiling potatoes 10 minutes. Cut into 1" slices, on the diagonal.

FINAL PROCEDURE:

Peel hot potatoes (by holding up with a fork or laying on flat surface). Set these aside. You will slice them right into the salad.

Salad Dressing: Pour off all but 4 tablespoons bacon grease from skillet. Place skillet over low heat. Stir in flour, sugar, salt, and pepper. Stir and blend together. Add water and vinegar. Cook, stirring, until thickened. (It should be the consistency of medium-thin gravy.)

To serve: Remove skillet from heat. Alternate in skillet layers of potato slices, frank slices, celery, romaine, cucumber, and onion rings. Toss salad carefully but quickly until it is well mixed. Crumble bacon over the top. Serve at once from the skillet. (Serves 6.)

Sean's Roast Rhinoceros (page 135) is also very good for parties

+ +

RTY #4 - PARTY #4 - PARTY #4 - PARTY #4 - PARTY #4 - PARTY #4 - PARTY #4 - PART

+ CHATTER +

If small "new" potatoes are used, they will cook in less time. Use 8 or 10 (depending on size), slice them directly into salad without paring.

+ +

PARTY #5 - PARTY #5 - PARTY #5 - PARTY #5 - PARTY #5 - PARTY #5 - PARTY #5 - PA

+ +

+ +

MENU (serves 6)

Shish Kebab
Kasha (Buckwheat Groats)
Slavic Potato Salad

+ +

+ SHISH KEBAB +

Preparation: 20 minutes
Cooking: 10 minutes

In Armenia it's called "shish kebab," in Russia "shashlik," but in any country it is skewered meat that has been marinated to a succulent tenderness and then broiled over a charcoal fire or under the broiler. Wonderful flavors mingle when the skewered (or pinned) meat chunks are alternated with various vegetables. Because of present meat prices, it would be best to wait for a lamb or beef sale before indulging yourself in this luxury. You will need to buy a pack of wood skewers, about 50¢ for 6.

INGREDIENTS:

2 1/2 to 3-lb. lamb or beef, cut in 1 1/2" cubes (tell butcher it's for kebabs)

2 cloves garlic, mashed
1/2 cup oil (peanut or corn)
1/4 cup lemon juice
1 teaspoon oregano
1 teaspoon salt
12 mushrooms
3 green peppers
3 tomatoes (optional)

The meat should marinate at least 2-3 hours before cooking.

In large mixing bowl: Put mashed garlic cloves. Add oil, lemon juice, oregano, and salt. Stir well together.

Add meat chunks. Stir around. Leave meat in this mixture several hours, remembering to stir it around again now and then.

Remove stems from mushroom caps. Remove seeds from green peppers. Allow 2 mushrooms per person. Cut green peppers into same size as meat chunks, allowing 3-4 pieces per person. Quarter tomatoes, if you're using them.

Thread meat onto skewers, alternating with mushrooms, peppers, tomato pieces. Set the skewers on bottom of roasting pan.

Preheat broiler. Set roasting pan 7" from heating element. Broil for 5 minutes. Turn each skewer gently. Broil on that side 5 minutes more. Serve immediately on mounds of kasha. (Serves 6.)

\+ + + + + + + + + + + + + +

\+ MORE SHISH-KEBAB DINNER COMBINATIONS +

Figure about 1/2 lb. meat per person.

\+ LAMB +

Marinated lamb cubes, canned pineapple chunks, stuffed green olives.

Marinated lamb cubes with fresh mushroom caps, squares of green pepper, quartered tomatoes, raw potato chunks.

Un-marinated lamb kidneys, cut in half, with bacon squares. Bacon will oil kidneys while broiling.

\+ BEEF +

Marinate beef cubes in red wine, chopped onion, thyme. Skewer with cherry tomatoes, mushroom caps, raw potato chunks. Brush with oil while grilling.

Small meatballs, small canned onions, cherry tomatoes. Brush with oil while grilling.

\+ LIVER +

Marinate chicken livers in A-1 Sauce for 20 minutes. Alternate with bacon squares, quartered apples.

Wrap bacon around un-marinated chicken livers. Skewer with pineapple chunks, brush with soy sauce while grilling.

\+ CHATTER +

1. Anything goes on a skewer in any combination that sounds good. Select foods which will cook at the same rate of speed, and brush raw fruits and vegetables with oil before grilling.
2. To serve: Place 1 or 2 skewers on each plate. Diners serve themselves by pushing everything off the skewer, at once, with a fork.
3. The traditional accompaniment to kebabs is kasha, next.
4. It is not important but may be interesting to note that this dish, reputed to have its origins in the Caucasian area, is also found under slightly different labels and guises in Yugoslavia, Iran, Turkey, and fabled Arabia.

+ KASHA (BUCKWHEAT GROATS) + Cooking: 20 minutes

A unusual flavor, delicate but definite. Most people enjoy it the first time and it's loaded with vitamins.

4 cups water
2 bouillon cubes
2 teaspoons salt
2 cups unwashed kasha (whole buckwheat groats)
Butter

In a medium saucepan, put water, bouillon cubes, salt. Bring to a high boil.

Pour in kasha so slowly that the boiling does not stop. Stir. Let it boil 1 minute, uncovered.

Cover. Lower heat. Simmer 15 minutes. Uncover. Fluff kasha with a fork to separate grains. Turn off heat.

Let it rest 5 minutes to let steam escape. Dab a little butter on each serving. (Serves 6.)

+ CHATTER +

1. To be fancier, you can first fry 1 slice chopped bacon in the saucepan. Remove. Saute 1/2 chopped onion, 1/2 chopped green pepper. Proceed with recipe above. Serve topped with crumbled bacon.

2. Pack leftover kasha into a shallow dish, pressing it tightly. Refrigerate overnight to harden. Next day, cut it into squares and fry in oil for breakfast.

+ + + + + + + + + + + + + +

+ SLAVIC POTATO SALAD +

This takes a little advance preparation. Just boil the potatoes early in the day. The final effect, filling and delicious. Serve it cold.

INGREDIENTS:

5 medium-size potatoes
2 small cucumbers
4 scallions (green onions)
1 small bag of radishes (optional)
1 pint sour cream
2 pints (2 lb.) cottage cheese
1/2 teaspoon salt
1/2 teaspoon pepper

In the morning: Boil potatoes for 30 minutes, or till fork tender. Drain. Refrigerate.

Two-3 hours before serving: Peel potatoes. Cut into large bite-size pieces. Place in big mixing bowl or salad bowl. Peel cucumbers. Slice thin. Add to potatoes.

Remove "beards" from scallions, and discard. Cut scallions into bowl using about 3/4 of the green parts, too. (If you're using radishes, wash, and slice them into bowl.)

Now add sour cream, cottage cheese, salt and pepper, and stir all together gently till well mixed. Taste. Add a bit more salt if necessary. REFRIGERATE. Serve very cold. (Serves 6-8.)

+ CHATTER +

This is usually served, as is, from the bowl. Or, if you wish, you can place each serving on a large lettuce leaf.

+ +

PARTY #6 - PARTY #6 - PARTY #6 - PARTY #6 - PARTY #6 - PARTY #6 - PARTY #6 - PA

+ +

+ +

MENU (serves 6) Very-Little-Coin Masterpiece
Caesar Salad

+ +

+ VERY-LITTLE-COIN MASTERPIECE +

Preparation: 30 minutes
Cooking: 40 minutes

This is the kind of open casserole dish that might be served to you in Switzerland or Aspen at an apres-ski party. It's hot sausage and sliced potatoes surrounded with a bubbling melted cheese sauce - inexpensive yet superb. Note: You will need a 9" x 13" x 2" baking dish. Measure your roasting pan. It should substitute nicely.

INGREDIENTS:

2 large onions
4 tablespoons (1/2 stick) butter or margarine
1 1/2 lb. kielbasi sausage (or Italian garlic type)
Three 1-lb. cans sliced white potatoes
4 eggs
2 cups (1 pint) light cream
1/2 teaspoon salt
1/4 teaspoon pepper
2 oz. (1/2 cup) grated Swiss cheese

PREPARATION:

Do this 2 hours before dinner: Peel and slice onions. Melt butter in skillet on medium heat. Add onions. Cook gently 4-5 minutes till onions are just tender but not browned. Stir a bit.

Slice sausage thickly (about 1"). Grease baking dish or roasting pan. Open and drain cans of potatoes.

Arrange cooked onions and sliced sausage and potatoes in concentric circles in greased baking dish.

In mixing bowl, beat together eggs, cream, salt and pepper till well mixed. Pour into baking dish, covering all ingredients with mixture.

Grate Swiss cheese. Sprinkle it on top. Refrigerate 1 hour.

Heat oven to 375. Bake the "Masterpiece" for 40 minutes. (Serves 6.)

+ + + + + + + + + + + + + + +

+ CAESAR SALAD + Preparation: 10 minutes

This world-famous salad is attributed to France, Italy, and everywhere, but the right place: a small hotel in Tijuana, Mexico - "Caesar's." Don't know where Caesar is today, but let us honor his inspiration by including it here for you. Wash, dry, and refrigerate lettuce ahead.

INGREDIENTS:

2 cloves garlic
1 small can anchovies
1/2 teaspoon pepper
6 tablespoons salad oil (peanut, corn)
2 tablespoons lemon juice
2 medium-size heads romaine lettuce
2 oz. (1/2 cup) grated Parmesan or Romano cheese
2 eggs
1/2 package croutons

PREPARATION:

In largest mixing bowl or salad bowl, put garlic cloves, peeled and sliced. Add anchovies (plus juice) and 1/2 teaspoon black pepper. With back of wooden spoon mash all together hard till it's a pulpy mess. Add salad oil and lemon juice. Stir till well blended.

Break lettuce leaves into bite-size pieces. Add to bowl. Mix. Sprinkle in grated cheese.

Break both eggs over lettuce and drop them in raw! (Ignore remarks of squeamish guests.) Mix thoroughly, 15 times at least, till all greens are coated and no trace of egg remains.

Add croutons. Toss again a few times, gently. (Taste for a small addition of salt, but it should not be necessary.) Serve immediately, cold and crisp. (Serves 6.)

+ CHATTER +

1. Fresh-grated (do-it-yourself) cheese is always best, but the prepared grated saves time and energy.

2. Croutons can be bought ready-made. Leftover croutons are good in soup.

+ +

MENU (serves 8)	Jack's Best Stew
	Hard Rolls or Crusty Bread
	Tossed Green Salad

+ +

See EXAM-WEEK Specials for Jack's Best Stew. Really good for a party. Serve with a simple tossed green salad (see below) and crusty bread or rolls heated 10 minutes in a 350 oven. The stew's a do-ahead dish - preparation 20 minutes, cooking 2 hours, 10 minutes reheating.

+ GREENS TOSSED IN FRENCH DRESSING +

INGREDIENTS:

1 bag fresh washed spinach
2 cucumbers (large)
1 bunch watercress or parsley
1-lb. can stringbeans

Break thick stems off spinach, break leaves into bite-size pieces in large bowl. Peel and slice cucumbers. Add to bowl. Chop up watercress or parsley and add to bowl.

Open can of stringbeans. Drain well. Add, as is, to bowl. Refrigerate.

DRESSING:

2 tablespoons cider or wine vinegar
6 tablespoons salad oil
1/2 teaspoon mustard
1/2 teaspoon salt

In small bowl, mix all above ingredients well. When dinner's ready, pour over greens in large bowl. Mix, tossing 15-20 times, till all greens are well coated with dressing.

+ +

+ +

DRINKS - DRINKS - DRINKS - DRINKS

+ +

+ STILL OF THE NIGHT RED WINE +

Serves: Plenty
Preparation: 10 minutes
Waiting: 15 days

This recipe results in a sweet (dangerously strong) genuine wine, but it isn't foolproof. Altitude, humidity, temperature, will make differences. It should be a perfectly clear ruby color when finished.

ASSEMBLE:

1 gallon bottle, or jug, with a slender neck
Aluminum foil
1 toy balloon (which will fit over the bottle's neck)
1 1/2 quarts (24 oz.) grape juice (such as Welch's)
5 cups sugar
1/2 teaspoon dry yeast
Water

Make a funnel out of doubled aluminum foil. Insert in bottle.

Pour sugar, yeast, then grape juice through this. Shake. Mix very well to dissolve sugar and yeast.

Fill bottle with water to 2" from top.

Prick end of balloon with a pin a few times. Put it over the bottle top. (The balloon keeps the wine clean, lets gases escape, and acts as your indicator.)

Place bottle in a cool, dark place. Do not handle, stir, or shake. The balloon will inflate, then should deflate, which means the wine is ready. Try it in about 2 weeks.

When wine is ready, carefully pour it into smaller, clean bottles, trying not to disturb the bottom sediment. (To avoid stirring sediment at all, use a siphon and gravity.)

+ CHATTER +

1. A good gallon container is an old cider bottle or plastic milk bottle with handle. Glass is preferred.
2. If wine isn't sweet enough for you, serve it as Sangria (next).

+ + + + + + + + + + + + + +

+ SANGRIA FOR 2 +

Preparation: 5 minutes

This mixture was improvised by Spanish peasants to lighten their rather rough homemade country wines. Served there, it never tastes the same twice, so make it to your own taste. Sangria is semisweet, fragrant, and makes one bottle of wine go a long way.

It has been observed that too much strong
red wine can make the world look
very peculiar.

+ +

LINE UP YOUR INGREDIENTS:

1/2 bottle (regular size) Claret or Chianti (or any cheap, tart, red wine)
1 sweet, seedless orange with rind, cut in chunks
1/2 lemon with rind, cut in chunks
1/4 cup sugar
1 cup club soda, or water
Ice

Pour wine into a pitcher. Add fruit chunks. Stir in sugar until dissolved. Refrigerate until serving time.

To serve: Add soda, ice, stir. Taste, add more sugar if you like.

+ CHATTER +

1. Substitute plain water for soda if you like, but soda makes Sangria a "sparkling" wine.

2. To make Sangria and serve at once: Pour wine into pitcher. Add sugar. Rapidly stir in a few ice cubes until wine is chilled. Add fruit (mashing it a bit first). Use less soda or water than in first recipe.

+ + + + + + + + + + + + + +

+ MIMI'S PERFECT ICED TEA +

Yield: 1/2 gallon
Preparation: 15 minutes

A sweet-tart blend more refreshing (and far cheaper) than any instant tea or soft drink. Nice to have around all the time.

ASSEMBLE:

One 1/2 gallon clean milk bottle, or a 1/2 gallon jug
Aluminum foil to form a funnel (or a funnel!)
5 Lipton tea bags (or any ordinary orange-pekoe type)
1/2 cup plus 2 tablespoons sugar
1/2 cup plus 2 tablespoons lemon juice (like Real Lemon in a bottle)
Water

Boil 3 cups water in medium saucepan. Add tea bags. Remove pan from heat, and let tea steep, covered, about 10 minutes.

Remove tea bags with slotted spoon, pressing gently first against side of pan. Discard bags.

Add sugar, stir till dissolved. Add lemon juice. Stir.

Pour tea essence into clean bottle, through funnel shaped of aluminum foil. Fill bottle with tap water to 2" from top. Refrigerate.

For Tea Ambrosia: Use 1/2 cup honey instead of sugar. Proceed as above. Drop 4-5 cloves into finished tea. Refrigerate. Shake bottle before pouring.

+ +

Just DESSERTS - Just DESSERTS -

+ +

HERE IS WHERE you get your just desserts, but if you want to make an elaborate one from scratch, you're looking in the wrong book. These are just a few recipes with special credentials - among them speed and efficiency.

If you've got the kind of sweet tooth that requires a big repertory of desserts, even the smallest grocery store has a dazzling display of cake mixes, puddings, etc., most of which are perfectly delicious - maybe not nutritious - but delicious.

+ +

+ STAPLES + It helps to have on hand just for DESSERTS:

Granulated sugar
Confectioners (powdered) sugar
Brown sugar
Hershey's cocoa
Vanilla extract
Baking soda
Powdered cinnamon
Honey
Maraschino cherries
Shelled walnuts
Strawberry jam

+ +

+ STEPHIE'S AMAZING BROWNIES +

Preparation: 15 minutes
Baking: 30 minutes

According to a recent survey, conducted at the dinner table, these brownies surpass any prepared mix going. One thing is certain, they're a lot cheaper. Recipe makes 9-12 brownies.

INGREDIENTS:

1 cup sugar
3/4 cup flour
1 stick (1/4 lb.) butter (or margarine)
5 tablespoons Hershey's cocoa
1/2 teaspoon salt
2 eggs
1 tablespoon vanilla extract
1/2 cup walnuts or pecans

PREPARATION:

Preheat oven to 350. Grease an 8" x 8" square cake pan. Chop nuts.

With wooden spoon, beat together all ingredients except nuts in large bowl 50 times.

Add nuts. Beat 10 times more. Pour into greased cake pan.

Put on center rack in oven. Bake 30 minutes. Leave in pan to cool. Serve from pan.

+ GRANNY'S CREAMY DREAMY CHEESE CAKE PIE +

Preparation: 15 minutes
Baking: 30 minutes
Refrigerate: several hours

Serves 8 or 16. This creamy, cold delight should be made several hours ahead or the day before to insure that it is icy cold. A cheese cake is usually served in slim wedges because it is so rich, therefore this quantity will serve 16 people. To serve 8, make it in two 8" pie pans, freeze one for later use. (See Chatter 1.)

INGREDIENTS FOR CRUST:

1/3 box Graham crackers, or use 2 cups pre-crushed Graham-cracker crumbs
1/4 lb. (1 stick) butter (or margarine)

Grease a 10" (or two 8") pie pans thoroughly inside with a piece of butter or margarine.

On flat clean surface: Use either rolling pin, bottle, or fists and fingers to pound Graham crackers till they're crushed fine. Measure 2 cups.

Melt stick of butter in skillet over medium heat. Remove from heat. Add Graham cracker crumbs. Stir to mix well.

Line the greased pie pan with crumb mixture on botton and sides. With back of spoon, press firmly to get it even all over.

INGREDIENTS FOR FILLING:

2 eggs
1 large and 1 small pkg. cream cheese (at room temperature)
1 pint (2 cups) sour cream
3/4 cups sugar
2 teaspoons vanilla extract

Preheat oven to 350.

In large mixing bowl, beat eggs till foamy. (Wire whisk does a good job.)

Add packs of soft cream cheese. Mash with fork till gloppy. Then stir and mash till egg is incorporated into cream cheese.

Add sour cream, sugar, and vanilla. Beat till soft and mixed, with very few lumps. Pour filling into crust of crumb mixture.

Bake on center rack of oven, at 350. Done in 30 minutes. Remove from oven. Let cool on counter for 1/2 hour. Refrigerate.

+ CHATTER +

1. To freeze soft-top cakes and pies without marring surface, freeze unwrapped. When rigid, wrap completely in foil.

2. To be extra fancy, top cheese cake with a couple of tablespoons of (thawed) frozen strawberries.

+ + + + + + + + + + + + + + +

+ MIAMI UNIVERSITY AMBROSIA +

Make this the night before. Twice as good next day. Even better for breakfast the day after that - if any's left over, which isn't too likely.

LINE UP YOUR INGREDIENTS - per person

1 1/2 navel oranges
1 teaspoon sugar, or to taste
2 heaping tablespoons canned shredded coconut (unsweetened)
1 miniature bottle orange liqueur (optional)

Peel oranges with sharp knife. Holding orange over soup plate or bowl, cut off all white stuff. Save juice that drips into bowl. Now slice oranges in bowl; more juice drips - save. Put slices in layers in some sort of serving bowl. Sprinkle sugar and half the coconut between layers. Sprinkle top with rest of coconut. Now pour over all about 1 teaspoon per orange of the orange liqueur. (maybe they don't do this at Miami U., but it's great.) Then add saved up orage juice. Cover. Refrigerate. Serve cold, cold, cold.

There's an Italian version of this: Substitute small jar of pine nuts for the coconut. Usually available in so-called gourmet corner of the supermarket.

+ + + + + + + + + + + + + +

+ JANE'S FLAMING BANANAS +

Preparation: 5 minutes
Cooking: 10 minutes

Serves 6. This arsonist's dream is luscious and showy. Try it, if only to prove you can make the best burnt bananas on the block.

LINE UP YOUR INGREDIENTS:

3 largest firm yellow bananas
2 tablespoons butter
2 tablespoons brown sugar
1/2 teaspoon cinnamon
1/4 cup (2 oz.) rum
1/2 pint vanilla ice cream

Start early in the day, if you wish. Peel bananas. Split in half, lengthwise.

In large (12") iron skillet over medium heat, melt butter till it bubbles. Add bananas. Cook 4 minutes on each side. (Turn gently, with spatula.) Remove from stove. Sprinkle with brown sugar and cinnamon, coating each banana lightly. Bananas can now sit and wait for dessert time.

To serve: In a small saucepan, on medium heat, warm rum till hot (but not boiling!).

Pour rum over bananas and ignite with match. Very effective. (DO NOT USE A CIGARETTE LIGHTER.) When flame dies, and applause ceases, serve each person half a banana topped with vanilla ice cream.

+ CHATTER +

1. If you find rum out of sight budget-wise, California brandy is low-priced and will do, though rum and bananas are traditional partners - it's a natural affinity. Or buy one of those miniature bottles - you need only 2 oz.

2. Helpful, but not imperative: If you remember, remove ice cream from freezer 10 minutes before it's needed, to soften.

3. Jane says you can ignite anything this way, and she does, from canned peaches, to baked apples, chicken, even a cake, by first warming the rum or brandy.

4. Jane is Dick's friend.

+ + + + + + + + + + + + + +

Refer to this one as . . .

+ "MY CHOCOLATE-CHERRY DUMP CAKE" +

Preparation: 30 minutes
Baking: 45 minutes

A real breakthrough here, folks! A fine cake you carelessly dump into a bowl, serve with a spoon. We include it because of its wondrous flavor - although the cake does seem to be too airy (or something) to come out of the pans properly and the frosting is too rich (or something) to spread. Anyway, it's a treat. Good exercise, too.

Preheat oven to 350.

Prepare cake tins: Two 9" x 9" or one 9" x 13" x 2". Coat inside with 1 tablespoon butter or oil. Dust with 1 tablespoon flour.

LINE UP YOUR INGREDIENTS:

15-oz. pkg. devil's-food cake mix (Duncan Hines, B. Crocker, etc.)
3-oz. pkg. cherry-flavor gelatin
2 tablespoons salad oil
1 cup water
3 eggs
4-oz. jar maraschino cherries

PREPARATION:

Drain cherry juice from jar. Save. Chop cherries (with scissors) into quarters or smaller. Save.

Into large mixing bowl, dump cake mix, gelatin, salad oil, and 1/2 cup of the water. Mix and beat this with a wooden spoon 100 times.

Add 2 eggs, one at a time. Beat 50 times after each egg.

Add half the chopped cherries, the 3rd egg, and the rest of the water. Beat 100 times or until it's all mixed. Pour batter into prepared cake pans (or pan).

Place in oven center. Bake 45 minutes at 350. (Meanwhile, make frosting.) Remove cake from oven. Let cool for 10 minutes.

Now dump half the cake into a large bowl, in chunks or however it comes out. Pour on half the frosting. Dump in rest of the cake, add rest of frosting. Decorate dramatically with last of the cherry bits.

+ CHOCOLATE-CHERRY FROSTING +

15-oz. pkg. dark chocolate (or fudge) frosting mix.
Maraschino cherry juice from bottle

Mix frosting to package directions, using butter, water, or whatever it calls for. Then add reserved bottled cherry juice. Mix in well. Distribute over Dump Cake as directed in cake recipe.

+ + + + + + + + + + + + + + +

+ CHRYSTIE'S ARABIAN FRUITY CAKE +

Preparation: 10 minutes
Cooking: 30-40 minutes

Serves 6-8. This one seems to be unique. It's close to a pure organic dessert, yet the flavor is subtly reminiscent of Arabian delights. WARNING: DO NOT SERVE CAKE WITHOUT ITS TOPPING. Their natural affinity for each other makes this the greatest!

INGREDIENTS FOR CAKE:

1 tablespoon butter
1 cup whole wheat flour (or white)
1/2 cup wheat germ
1/2 cup honey
1/2 cup brown sugar
1-lb. can fruit cocktail
1 egg
1 teaspoon baking soda

Preheat oven to 350. Grease a 9" x 9" cake pan with the butter.

In mixing bowl, mix and beat together the flour, wheat germ, honey, and brown sugar.

Open fruit cocktail. Drain off juice. Holding large sieve over mixing bowl, strain fruit through, pressing with back of wooden spoon. Mix fruit into flour mixture.

In a small bowl, beat egg till well mixed. Add to flour mixture. Add baking soda. Stir all well together. Pour into greased cake pan.

Put in oven on center rack, and bake 30-40 minutes, till golden brown and springy to the touch.

The cake can be served warm or cold, with warmed topping.

TOPPING:

1 stick butter
1 cup brown sugar
2 teaspoons vanilla extract
1/2 cup (buy small can) Carnation Evaporated milk

Put all topping ingredients in small saucepan. Stir over medium heat till it thickens (5-8 minutes). Leave in saucepan and reheat over medium heat whenever needed.

+ CHATTER +

Sprinkle leftover wheat germ on cereal every morning.

+ + + + + + + + + + + + + + +

+ MICHAEL'S SEWANEE SKILLET UPSIDE-DOWN CAKE +

Preparation: 10 minutes
Cooking: 40 minutes

Serves 8-10. Light and fluffy, sticky and sweet, this cake from the University of the South isn't a bit technical. It's made and baked in the same pan, and "turns out" every time. Try it. A beautiful cake, pre-decorated with brown-sugar-glazed fruits.

LINE UP YOUR INGREDIENTS:

1/2 cup (1 stick) butter
2 cups brown sugar
1-lb. can sliced pineapple
1 small jar maraschino cherries
4 oz. (1/2 cup) walnuts
2 cups Jiffy mix
1/4 cup toasted wheat germ
3/4 cup white sugar
1 egg
3/4 cup milk
2 tablespoons butter
1 teaspoon vanilla extract

GLAZE TOPPING:

In large (12") iron skillet, melt butter over medium heat. Remove to counter. Stir in brown sugar till well mixed. Spread evenly over skillet bottom.

Drain pineapple. Arrange slices artistically on brown sugar; this bottom part will become the cake top. Put in some whole rounds, some cut in halves. Open cherries. Use 10 or 12, split in half. Dot around sugar. Chop walnuts coarsely. Sprinkle over brown sugar.

CAKE BATTER:

Preheat oven to 375.

In large mixing bowl, stir together Jiffy mix, wheat germ, and white sugar. Add egg and milk. Stir.

Melt butter over medium heat. Add to mixture. Stir. Measure in vanilla.

Beat till light, about 200 strokes. Pour batter into skillet over fruit and brown sugar.

Bake on center rack of oven for 30 minutes. Test doneness by inserting a toothpick into cake center. If it comes out clean, cake is done. If not, return to oven 5-10 minutes more. Remove from oven. Let stand to cool for 5-10 minutes.

Now you test your steadiness as you proceed to turn the cake upside-down. Here's how: Put an extra-large plate upside-down on top of skillet. Hold skillet handle in one hand and hold plate covering skillet firmly with the other hand. Turn over. Let plate rest on table with skillet upside-down on top of it. Soon cake will gently plop down. Lift off skillet. Presto!

\+ + + + + + + + + + + + + +

\+ CHRIS'S ENGLISH TRIFLE OR GODDARD GLOP +

Preparation: 10 minutes
Cooking: 0
Refrigeration: 4 hours

Serves 6-8. This must be made in advance; at least 4 hours. It can be put together in a bread pan, casserole, or any deep dish. It needs no cooking and hardly any mixing. If you'd like a cool, smooth quickie, try it.

INGREDIENTS:

1-lb. pound cake
Strawberry jam
1 pkg. instant vanilla pudding
Milk
2 bananas
1 large jar maraschino cherries
6 oz. shelled walnuts
3 tablespoons sherry wine (optional)

PREPARATION:

Cut enough cake into 1/2" slices to line bottom of pan. (You will only need about half the cake for this. Use remainder another night, topped with ice cream and sauce.)

Spread cake slices with jam. Put on pan bottom, jam-side up.

In mixing bowl, mix instant pudding with milk according to package directions.

Peel bananas and slice 1/4" thick. Open and drain cherries. Cut into quarters (with scissors).

If you're using sherry wine, sprinkle it over the cake and jam, now.

Smear cake with half the vanilla pudding. Add a layer of sliced bananas and some of the quartered cherries.

Chop up walnuts. Sprinkle half of them on the banana layer.

Plop on another layer of vanilla pudding. Add the rest of the bananas. Add almost all the cherries and walnuts, but reserve a bit of each for the topping. Use the last vanilla pudding to cover. Sprinkle top with the leftover cherries and walnuts.

Refrigerate half a day, at least. To serve: Just scoop out with a spoon. Trying to cut, like cake, is hopeless.

\+ + + + + + + + + + + + + +

+ +

Hey man! Don't you know you gotta get some FOOD in here before exams?

+ +

EXAM-WEEK Specials - EXAM-WEEK Specials

+ +

It is vital that you have filling, nutritious food handy, always ready, during the demanding days and crazy time schedules of EXAM WEEK. Here are several recipes that will feed you throughout that period. Select one, make it a day in advance, buy some fresh fruit, and 2 of you won't go hungry for the number of days indicated . . .

That Pork and Sauerkraut Dish of Marian's - 3 days
Easy Rider Casserole - 3 or 4 days
Jack's Best Stew - 3 or 4 days
Hero Hash, Open-Face - 3 or 4 days
Sean's Roast Rhinoceros - 4 days
McCrystle's Survival Casserole (page 40) - doubled, 3 days
Meat Loaf (page 90) - doubled, 2 days (bake in 12" skillet)

+ +

+ THAT PORK AND SAUERKRAUT DISH OF MARIAN'S +

Preparation: 1/2 hour
Cooking: 2 hours

Don't pass this one by! Even if you think you hate sauerkraut, make it anyway. It's a series of taste sensations which never become tiresome as they change with each day's new meat additions. Word has it, some people have kept it going for years! Here's your chance to be inventive. You'll need a heavy, large (8-quart) casserole with lid. Should last 3 days for 2.

LINE UP YOUR INGREDIENTS:

2-lb. pork loin (boneless)
1 lb. kielbasi (Polish sausage)
4 knockwurst frankfurters
4 medium onions
3 tablespoons butter
1-lb. can tomatoes
1-lb. can tomato sauce
2-lb. can sauerkraut
1 small head cabbage
3 medium potatoes
1 medium apple
2 teaspoons basil
2 teaspoons marjoram
10 peppercorns

Peel and slice onions. Slice pork loin in wide (2") chunks.

In large skillet, melt butter. Add pork to brown. After 5 minutes, turn pork over. Add onions to brown. After 5 more minutes, transfer pork, onions, and skillet juices to the large casserole. Add can of tomatoes, tomato sauce, and sauerkraut. Stir.

Slice cabbage thin. Peel and slice potatoes thin. Cut apple in large chunks chunks, removing core; leave peel on. Add cabbage, potatoes, and apple to big casserole. Now add all spices - basil, marjoram, and peppercorns.

Fold things over. Bring to boil, then lower to simmer. Cover and cook for

1 hour. After 1 hour, bury kielbasi deep in pot. Cook 1 more hour.

The first night eat the pork loin, the second, the kielbasi. The third night, add the 4 plump knockwurst, and eat them. Serve with mustard, or ketchup, or both. Each night before eating, reheat over medium heat for 15-20 minutes. No more cooking required.

+ + + + + + + + + + + + + +

+ EASY RIDER CASSEROLE +

Preparation: 45 minutes
Cooking: About 2 hours

A student from the University of Santo Domingo, Alejandro, contributed his country's native dish, a stew called Casido. It's a tasty lot of fun, goes on for 4 nights to serve 2. You will need a large stove-top casserole or Dutch oven, about a 8-quart size will do nicely.

BASIC INGREDIENTS FOR FIRST 2 DAYS:

3-lb. fryer chicken, cut up
2 lb. shins of beef
1- 1 1/2-lb. kielbasi-type sausage
4 medium potatoes
1/2 head of cabbage
3 tablespoons oil or bacon fat
2 cans garbanzos (chick peas)
1 large onion
2 garlic cloves
1 tablespoon tomato paste
Some salt and pepper

PREPARATION:

Wash and pat dry chicken pieces. Peel potatoes, cut in half. Cut the half head cabbage into big chunks (reserve the other half). Likewise, onion and garlic.

Heat oil in casserole over medium heat. Brown chicken parts in hot oil, about 10 minutes each side. Remove chicken to nearby platter.

Brown pieces of shin of beef in same oil (add 1-2 more tablespoons oil if needed), about 5 minutes per side.

Now return chicken to casserole. Add onion, garlic, and tomato paste. Measure enough water into casserole to barely cover meat.

Bring to boil over high heat. Cover. Turn heat to low. Simmer for 1 hour.

Then add kielbasi sausage, whole, plus cabbage and potatoes. Continue cooking uncovered, at a slow bubbly simmer for 30 minutes.

Add 1 can of garbanzos with juice. (Reserve other can.) Cook another 15 minutes.

Before serving, remove the shins of beef and kielbasi sausage to a bowl. Refrigerate for other nights.

The FIRST night: Eat the chicken with half the vegetables.

The SECOND night: Heat up the shins of beef in the casserole over medium heat, covered, for 10 minutes. Serve with remaining vegetables. Save the broth in the casserole.

The THIRD night: Cut up other 1/2 head of cabbage, 2-3 washed carrots, and put in broth in casserole. Cook, covered, on low heat, 30 minutes.

Next add: Second can of garbanzos plus a handful of noodles and the kielbasi sausage, cut into 2" chunks. Reheat on low heat, covered, 10 minutes or till noodles are cooked. Save broth again.

The FOURTH night: Add to the broth, 1 lb. hamburger meat, 2-3 medium potatoes, peeled and cut into dice-size pieces, 1 mashed clove garlic, 1 teaspoon oregano (and, if you like things peppery, 2-3 drops Tabasco or 1/2 teaspoon black pepper).

If juice in casserole was less than a cup, add water. Bring to a boil. Cover. Simmer 20 minutes. Add 1/2 teaspoon salt, or enough to zip up, and serve.

This really should be the end of the Casido AND of your exams!

+ CHATTER +

Please note: By the third and fourth nights, you must be prepared to buy a pound of fresh hamburger, some noodles, as well as have carrots, garlic, potatoes, and maybe a bottle of Tabasco on hand.

+ + + + + + + + + + + + + +

+ JACK'S BEST STEW +

Preparation: 20 minutes
Cooking: 2 hours

Although this has 16 ingredients, note that most of them just drop in, with little chopping involved. So, you easily create a filling, superbly flavored stew. If there's lots of gravy, eat the stew in the old-fashioned way, in soup bowls, with chunks of crusty bread or rolls to sop it up. Should last 3 days for 2; see CHATTER.

INGREDIENTS:

4 lb. stewing beef (2" cubes)
4 tablespoons flour
1/4 cup cooking oil
2 tablespoons lemon juice
1 tablespoon Worcestershire sauce
2 cloves garlic, chopped
1 large onion, chopped
4 bay leaves
2 teaspoons sugar
2 teaspoons salt
1/2 teaspoon pepper
1 tablespoon paprika
2 dashes ground cloves
8 carrots, quartered
Two 1-lb. cans Irish potatoes
1-lb. can white onions.

Cut excess fat (but not all of it) off beef cubes. Shake beef in paper bag with flour till well-coated.

In large (12") skillet, heat oil. Brown beef over medium-high heat.

In saucepan, bring 1 quart (4 cups) water to boil. Transfer stew beef to large stew pot. Add boiling water. Add all other ingredients except carrots, canned potatoes, and onions.

Bring to a boil over high heat. Turn to low. Cover. Simmer for about 2 hours, or till beef is tender.

Cut carrots in quarters. Drain cans of potatoes and onions. Twenty minutes before stew is done, add carrots.

When stew is cooked, remove from heat. Add canned potatoes and onions. Just before dinner, reheat for 10 minutes.

+ CHATTER +

This stew will stretch - that's what stews are supposed to do. Since there are 4 pounds of meat here, you should be able to keep it going to a fourth day by having in reserve: 1 box whole frozen string beans, 1 can red kidney beans, beans, and a 1/2" thick slice precooked ham. Rinse kidney beans in sieve. Cut ham in small chunks. Dump all 3 new ingredients into pot, add a bit of water if gravy level is low, and reheat on medium 15 minutes.

+ + + + + + + + + + + + + + +

+ HERO HASH, OPEN-FACE +

Preparation: 30 minutes
Cooking: 20 minutes

A version of the famous Italian Grinder, or Hero, sandwich, this juicy mixture lasts for days, improving with time and your own creative additions.

INGREDIENTS:

8 plump Italian sausages
2 lb. ground chuck
1 large onion
3 large cloves garlic
2 large green peppers
2 large tomatoes
1 tablespoon oregano
1 teaspoon salt
1 cup Uncle Ben's converted rice

Check each night for additional underlined ingredients.

PREPARATION:

Cut off 4 sausage links and refrigerate for another night. Remove sausage meat from skin (casing) of remaining 4. (To do this, cut off tip of sausage at one end and squeeze out meat like toothpaste from a tube.)

Put meat in large (12") skillet over medium heat. Cook, stirring, 5 minutes.

Meanwhile, slice and chop the onion, garlic, and green peppers. Add vegetables to skillet. Saute 3-4 minutes, stirring occasionally.

Add ground chuck. Cook, turning now and then, till pink disappears (3-4 minutes). Cut tomatoes into eighths and add to skillet. Measure in oregano and salt. Stir all well to blend.

Cover skillet. Simmer on low heat for 20 minutes.

Meanwhile, cook 1 cup of rice in 2 cups of boiling water (with 1 teaspoon salt). Cover, turn down to simmer on low heat. Cook 20 minutes, or till rice is dry and water disappears.

The FIRST night: Serve Hero Hash on rice.

The SECOND night: Mix leftover rice into leftover Hero Hash. Cover. Reheat on low for 10 minutes. Stir once or twice to heat evenly.

The THIRD night: Use last 4 Italian sausages, skinned and cooked in skillet the same way as first night for 5 minutes. Drain a 1-lb. can white beans (save juice). Add beans to skillet. Stir in leftover hash, plus enough bean juice to moisten. Mix together. Cover. Simmer on low heat 15 minutes. A can of cold asparagus or a green salad is good with this.

The FOURTH night: 1) Add 1 can sliced potatoes and 2 tomatoes, cut up, to leftover Hero Hash in skillet. Cook, covered, over low heat 10 minutes.
OR, 2) Add a 1-lb. can or jar of favorite spaghetti meat sauce to Hero Hash in skillet. Cover. Cook 15 minutes on medium-low heat. Serve on small loaves of Italian bread, cut in half lengthwise. Behold. Grinders!

\+ CHATTER +

1. Instead of rice the first night, you can cook bulgur (cracked wheat). Cooks like rice; see directions on package.
2. Fourth night, any cooked leftover meat or fowl you may have in refrigerator, chop up and add to skillet. Works fine.

\+ + + + + + + + + + + + + +

\+ SEAN'S ROAST RHINOCEROS +

Thawing: Overnight
Preparation: Zero
Cooking: 3-4 hours

What? No rhinoceros at your supermarket? Well, OK, of course not. But down at the end of the frozen-meats counter are large, lumpish things in plastic bags at low, low prices per pound and often on sale. Not rhinoceri, but turkeys!

The serving of turkey is usually - still - surrounded by ancient rites practiced when a 40-pound bird was barely enough to feed the assembled clan. While everybody is joyously cocktailing and throwing Frisbees in the yard, Mother, the sorceress, is back in the kitch. Intent, flushed, and sweating, she is doing mystic things - stuffing, trussing, basting, peering, also poking. She might as well be roasting a rhinoceros, but she is not in fact cooking anything unique - just a readily available, cheap, previously frozen, ordinary turkey. All she really has to do is FOLLOW THE DIRECTIONS ON THE PACKAGE (e.g., roasting time).

PROCEDURE:

All you have to do is to buy one of those frozen turkeys of a weight between 10 and 12 pounds only. No more. This will feed 2 people meat for lunch and dinner both for up to 4 days.

Thaw it overnight in sink. Remove exterior and interior bags. Dry creature inside and out with paper towels. Place in large roasting pan, chest side up. Tie ends of legs together with string if you want (elastic band will NOT do). Shove in 325 oven. Roasting time will be 3 to 4 hours. Don't baste it; at this weight, it shouldn't need it. Beast is tender when a leg moves easily in joint.

Remove bird to platter. Let it sit on counter 15-20 minutes. Eat it.

+ CHATTER +

1. You think all that is too simple? All right. See a few refinements of bird roasting under Roast Chicken, page 95. You can also make Giblet Gravy. See Chicken Giblet Gravy, page 96. Handy for fixing leftovers.

2. Getting tired of cold turkey? See Roast Chicken Leftovers beginning on page 98.

3. All those enormous bones? See Survival Bone Soup, page142.

+ + + + + + + + + + + + + + +

French chef's nightmare during his exam week.

+ +

+ +

FLAT-BROKE Specials

+ +

THESE FOODS may not be elaborate enough to present to the Shah of Iran the next time he drops in, but they are all low-cost and good tasting and that's the point.

+ +

We also suggest these CHEAPIES . . .

Touchdown Tuna Casserole (page 44)
Creamy Ham and Macaroni Casserole (page 94)
Don't-Clam-Up Spaghetti (page 62)

And see SURVIVAL!, next chapters.

+ +

+ JON'S CHICKEN SPARERIBS +

Preparation: 5 minutes
Marinating: 15 minutes (or all day)
Cooking: 45 minutes

Serves 2. This cheap and easy chicken dish comes out brown and succulent. Eat it with your fingers, go Oriental with a side bowl of rice. Note that you can cook at once; or prepare in the a.m. and let wings sit in the marinade all day.

LINE UP YOUR INGREDIENTS:

1 1/2 to 2 lb. chicken wings
1/4 cup soy sauce
1/2 cup Boone's Farm Apple Wine, or honey
Some butter

PREPARATION:

Under cold tap water, wash chicken wings. Dry well.

In mixing bowl, measure the soy sauce, apple wine or honey. Stir well.

Add chicken wings to this marinade, and let sit at room temperature at least 15 minutes, but the longer the better.

Preheat oven to 400. Grease large (12") skillet with a bit of butter.

Place chicken wings flat, not overlapping, in skillet. Spoon 2-3 tablespoons of marinade over chicken.

Place in oven. Bake 15 minutes. Baste wings with 2-3 more tablespoons of marinade, and bake 15 minutes more. Repeat basting process again, bake another 15 minutes (45 minutes in all).

Serve with, or on top of . . .

+ RICE +

Bring to boil 1 cup Uncle Ben's converted rice in 2 cups water. Turn to low heat, and simmer, covered, 20 minutes.

Add 1 tablespoon butter. Stir and serve, or keep warm, by covering, till wings are done.

\+ + + + + + + + + + + + + +

+ POOR BOY'S SOUP +

Rich in calcium, amino acids, and B vitamins, beans return to you far more than you pay out for them, and that's a bargain any time. This recipe will feed 2 people for 2 or 3 meals, with a total coin outlay of less than a dollar.

INGREDIENTS:

- 1-lb. pkg. white beans (navy or pea)
- 1 or 2 smoked ham hocks (if unavailable, use bacon, or bacon fat)
- 2 large onions
- 2 cloves garlic
- 2 stalks celery and leaf tops
- 1/2 teaspoon basil (optional)
- 3 big carrots (optional)
- 3 tablespoons parsley (optional)
- Salt and pepper

When possible, use all the listed ingredients, but at the very least, use the first 4.

Rinse dried beans in sieve. Put in large soup pot. Add 2 quarts (8 cups) water.

Peel and cut up onions and garlic cloves. Add to pot. If you are using smoked ham hocks, put them in now. Also celery, parsley, and basil.

Bring water to rapid boil over high heat. Cover. Turn to low heat. Simmer for 2 hours.

Wash carrots. Remove root ends. (Don't peel.) Slice thin. Add to soup. (If you have not used ham hocks, now's the time to also add 6 slices bacon cut up, or 3 tablespoons bacon fat.

Cook, covered, 20 minutes more. Taste with wooden spoon. Add salt. One teaspoon salt plus 1/2 teaspoon pepper should be plenty.

+ CHATTER +

1. Contrary to some directions, beans should not always be presoaked overnight. If they are, save the soaking water and use it in the soup as the water contains many of the B vitamins.
2. This recipe is equally delicious if you substitute dried lentils or dried split peas for the white beans.
3. For variety: Second night, add a can of stewed or plain tomatoes and heat 10 minutes, covered.

+ SPAGHETTI MYSTERIOSO +

Preparation: 10 minutes
Cooking: 50 minutes

Six big servings costing about 30¢ each! This tastes like a fine spaghetti with meat sauce and was invented by mountain folk of Sicily who seldom eat meat because they're flat broke. (Don't tell anyone it contains eggplant and no one will ever guess.)

LINE UP YOUR INGREDIENTS:

2 garlic cloves
1-lb. eggplant
1/2 cup cooking oil
Two (1-lb.) cans tomatoes
2 green peppers
3 teaspoons oregano (heaping)
1 teaspoon salt (heaping)
1/2 teaspoon pepper (heaping)
1 lb. spaghetti (thin, e.g. spaghettini)

SAUCE:

The sauce can be put together in 10 minutes if you've learned how to chop round objects (page 24): Peel and dice garlic cloves. Peel and dice eggplant (as you would an onion). Open tomato cans.

In large (12") skillet, heat oil over medium heat. Cook garlic pieces 1 minute or until just golden.

Add diced eggplant, then tomatoes and their juice. Stir well, breaking up tomatoes. While this cooks, wash green peppers, cut in half, remove seeds. Slice and dice peppers, stir them in at once.

Let mixture come to a good boil, over high heat, then turn down to medium heat. Cover pan, simmer, stirring occasionally, 30 to 40 minutes or until eggplant is soft and mushy.

Add seasonings - oregano, salt, and pepper.

Stir well and cook 10 more minutes. Serve over spaghetti.

SPAGHETTI:

Fifteen minutes before sauce is ready, get 6 to 8 cups salted water boiling in large saucepan. Add spaghetti. Stir to separate. Cook until just tender, 8 minutes (taste it).

To serve: Drain spaghetti. Pour half the sauce into a large casserole or the roasting pan. Add spaghetti and rest of sauce. Clean skillet with 1/4 cup water, add to sauce. Mix very well with a couple of spoons. Serve.

+ CHATTER +

1. Reheat in small quantities in a saucepan, or in oven, stirring in a teaspoon of water if it seems dry.

2. This is one spaghetti which doesn't seem to call for grated cheese, but chunks of a hard-crust bread are a nice addition.

3. To prepare this the authentic Sicilian way: Use just 1/2 teaspoon salt in sauce. For last 10 minutes of cooking, add 3 anchovy fillets, minced; 1 tablespoon capers; 1/2 cup sliced Italian black olives. But the recipe doesn't have to have all these rarities to make it good.

+ + + + + + + + + + + + + +

THE VALUE OF SOYBEANS cannot be overemphasized. A true meat substitute, they contain twice as much protein as meat or fish, 3 times as much as eggs, 11 times the amount in milk. They also abundantly contain essential amino acids, calcium, and the B vitamins. They are bean-cheap, and can be deliciously prepared. You can cook the dried bean (an overnight endeavor); or sprout soybean sprouts yourself (about 3 days); or buy beans cooked and canned (plain or in sauce). Here's how:

+ COOKED SOYBEANS +

Put 1 cup dried soybeans in refrigerator ice tray. Cover with 2 cups water. Freeze overnight.

Next day: Remove from refrigerator and drop, frozen, into largest saucepan. Add 1 1/2 cups water. Bring to boil. Turn to low. Cover. Simmer 2 1/2 to 3 hours, or till tender.

Add the following:

2 tablespoons oil (peanut, corn)
2 chopped garlic cloves
1 large chopped onion
1 teaspoon lime juice
1/2 teaspoon salt
3 tablespoons ketchup
1 tablespoon Worcestershire sauce

Cook, uncovered, over medium heat till all liquid is absorbed, 30-45 minutes. Serve sprinkled with chopped parsley, or plain. Serves 2.

+ + + + + + + + + + + + + +

+ SOY SUEY +

Buy "sprouting soybeans." Follow package directions. In 3 days you'll have fresh sprouts. Serve in salads - or, cook as follows:

INGREDIENTS:

3 tablespoons oil
1 green pepper, chopped
3 celery stalks, chopped
1 clove garlic, chopped
2-3 cups bean sprouts

Heat oil in large (12") skillet. Add all chopped ingredients. Cook over medium heat, stirring a bit, 5 minutes. Add bean sprouts. Cover. Cook 10 more minutes. Season with 1 teaspoon soy sauce or 1/2 teaspoon salt. Serve plain, or over boiled rice. Serves 2.

SURVIVAL

+ +

SURVIVAL! SURVIVAL! SURVIVAL!

+ +

ONCE UPON A TIME during World War II, a mean old Witch who lived in the Phillipines went to the right Government Office and agreed to care for 6 orphaned children. She had heard that Uncle Sam paid good money to foster parents and wanted to get in on the deal. She swore piously that she would care for them "as if they were her very own." But she didn't.

Back in the weird shack on the shore, her own children sat down to marvelous hamburgers in thick buns, french-fried potatoes, and gooey desserts (paid for with the money she had received), but the orphans got only hasty handouts of the cheap bread she made herself, and thin soups the Witch threw together from fish heads, chewed chicken bones, cut-rate vegetables, things like that.

At the end of 4 years, the foster children were tall, beautiful, royal-looking, with glossy hair and clear whites of the eyes; while her own children were fat, listless, with sensational acne complexions.

A social worker, too late, told her what was wrong. The cheap bread and garbage soup she had fed the orphans were loaded with the vitamins, minerals, and protein which her own childrens' diet lacked.

This happens to be a true story. The moral of it is this: You, too, should make Survival Bread and Survival Bone Soup to save money and get royal-looking.

+ +

+ SURVIVAL BONE SOUP +

Essentially, this is garbage soup. It's every bone and vegetable or salad scrap left on your plate. It's potato peelings, tomato tops, wilted lettuce leaves (yes, wash them), leftover pan or skillet drippings, and vegetable juices drained from cooked or canned vegetables.

No matter how far-out this sounds, honestly, it's fantastically good, so rich it forms a jelly when refrigerated, and contains, in 1 serving, the calcium equivalent of 3 quarts of milk!

OK, so there is a small catch to this miracle. If you don't drink it all up, you MUST, repeat MUST, bring this concoction to a boil about every 3 days, maybe 4, to be absolutely certain it will not ferment. Instead of making a chore of this, why not just automatically have some hot soup every few days? Just boil it up, have some, and if there's not much left, add it to a new batch of bones and vegetable leftovers and start all over again. This thing goes on forever.

PROCEDURE:

Put all your bones in the largest saucepan. (If your butcher will kindly give or sell you a fresh pig's foot or two, split, be grateful.) Add 8 cups of water, 2 teaspoons of salt, and 1/4 cup vinegar. (Vinegar is essential, and not as wild as it sounds. It draws out precious bone calcium. Its odor and taste dispel in cooking.) Throw in any leftover vegetable bits and pieces.

Bring to a boil. Turn down to low. Cover, and simmer 5 hours. Leave as is, on counter, overnight, with lid sort of askew.

Next day, skim off top grease with a spoon. At sink, strain soup through sieve into large bowl. Throw out bones, etc., but put back any good meat, and add those vegetable juices you saved.

You can eat this immediately.

Or, you can save it, have it later, perhaps adding bits of leftover chopped-up meat, tomatoes, celery, or whathaveyou - which you cook only 15 minutes in it. To what's left over, throw in from time to time more scraps, pan drippings (see CHATTER), vegetable juices. After 2-3 days of this nonsense, you'll have a soup of ever-changing, marvelous flavors.

+ CHATTER +

Pan drippings: Every time you've fried meat in a skillet or roasted it, surely you've noticed a residue clinging to pan bottom? That's essence of nutrition! If you're not making gravy with it, how to trap it? Just add 1/4 cup of water to pan, heat and stir a minute to loosen all particles, and dump into your Survival Bone Soup. (This also helps to clean pan.)

+ + + + + + + + + + + + + +

+ SURVIVAL BREAD +

We have 2 nephews who made over $250 apiece summers making and selling bread from this Parker family recipe. They mixed it in the evening, completed it the next morning. But the job can be finished in 3-4 hours if you prefer. Speedy rising time depends upon the amount of yeast used.

Unlike most bread formulas, this requires very little "kneading" (punching the dough around). However, after the dough has risen for the first time it has a great feel - like a little pillow - and you can play with it as much as you like (just keep it clean). You can make Herb Bread or Cinnamon Raisin Bread from the same recipe.

If you make this with stone-ground flour and milk, it is truly a staff-of-life food, unlike the edible paper now sold under the name "enriched bread." "Enriched" is one of those Orwell-1984 terms which mean just the opposite. Three nutrients are added to flour to replace the 22 previously removed. Why were they removed? Wheat products containing the entire wheat germ attract bugs (weevils, etc.) and "spoil" while on the grocer's shelf. Today, only man will eat "enriched" flour. Weevils, with their instinctive survival habits, won't touch it. But you can use regular flour and plain water and produce a good-tasting bread.

Yeasts were first discovered in ancient Egypt and were, of course, considered magic. Even today the Mexican word for yeast is "alma," meaning "spirit" and the breads you make will become better and better and rise faster because of the invisible wild yeast which will multiply in your own kitchen. How about that!

+ 4-HOUR SURVIVAL BREAD +

Preparation: 30 minutes in all

This is the whole thing: Mix dough in a bowl and let it rise about 2 hours. Then divide dough into loaf pans, let it rise 1 hour more. Bake it about 40 minutes. Makes 2 or 3 loaves.

YOU NEED:

A measuring cup
A coffee cup
A teaspoon
A big mixing bowl
Clean hands
A clean surface to work on

LINE UP YOUR INGREDIENTS:

1/4 cup sugar
1/4 cup warm water
2 packages dry yeast
2 cups warm milk (or water)
6 cups flour
1 tablespoon salt
1/2 stick (1/4 cup) soft butter

MAKE YEAST MIXTURE. Run tap water until it feels nice and warm, but not hot, on the inside of your wrist. Put first 3 ingredients into a coffee cup, stir. Let this mixture sit and get foamy, about 10 minutes. Meanwhile:

HEAT MILK IN SAUCEPAN OVER LOW HEAT. You want it the same warm temperature as the water. If it gets too hot, cool it.

MEASURE LEVEL CUPS OF FLOUR INTO A BIG BOWL. Don't shake it down too much, level off each cupful with the back of a knife.

ADD SALT: Mix through flour.

ADD BUTTER. Room-temperature butter is easier to handle but cold butter is OK. With both hands rub butter into flour until it disappears and all has a silky feel.

POUR IN YEAST MIXTURE.

ADD WARM MILK. With one hand pouring, the other squishing, gradually add milk to flour. You are trying to wet all dry ingredients. It will be terribly sticky. Have courage!

MIX ALL WELL. With both hands turn the mass over and over, in and out, until excess flour is incorporated. It will end up as a round sticky ball, or a round smooth ball, depending on the humidity. Either is fine.

COVER BOWL WITH A DAMP KITCHEN TOWEL. Run a clean towel under warm tap water, wring out. Stretch smooth over bowl.

PLACE BOWL IN A WARM PLACE. Use any place that is out of drafts and continuously warm. If you have no such place try: 1) The back of an electric stove top with front 2 burners turned on low. Or 2) If stove is gas, place over center pilot light on stove top. Or 3) Inside an electric oven which has been heated to 200, turned off, cooled 5 minutes. Keep oven door closed. Or 4) Inside a gas oven which has a permanently lit pilot light.

LET DOUGH RISE TO TWICE ITS ORIGINAL SIZE. About 2 hours.

GREASE INSIDES OF 2 OR 3 BREAD LOAF PANS. Use butter or cooking oil. Some people make 3 loaves because they prefer a slightly smaller loaf - or want to have more to sell.

PREPARE WORKING SURFACE. Any place that's clean, flat, convenient to clean up. Plastic or wood surfaces are both fine. You can adapt to either. Put some flour on wood surface to prevent dough sticking.

TURN OUT DOUGH. Poke finger into dough center. It will deflate. Scoop out all dough and dump it on the clean surface. With floured hands, pat dough flat. Then fold it over and over like a letter. If it feels sticky, flour your hands again, sprinkle a small amount of flour on dough. Knead this way 8 to 10 times until it feels like a foam-rubber pillow, is easy to handle.

CUT DOUGH IN HALF. As evenly as possible with a long knife.

FORM EACH HALF INTO A LOAF. Either pat, form, and stretch it into a smooth cylinder; or, pat and roll flat (with rolling pin or bottle), then roll tightly like a jelly roll.

PUT IN GREASED NARROW PANS. Loaves should be long enough to touch both narrow ends of pan, but do not have to touch long sides. If dough was rolled, place seam side down.

COVER LOAF PANS WITH DAMP CLOTH, LET RISE AGAIN. Return them to that warm place until dough has doubled in size again. About 45 minutes. The higher part of the dough should be level with the pan top.

PREHEAT OVEN TO 400.

BAKE BREAD. On center rack, about 35-40 minutes.

TEST IF BREAD IS DONE. It should have pulled away from the sides. Empty it from the pan, thump bottoms with fingers. It should have a hollow sound. If not, put back for a few minutes.

COOL BREAD ON WIRE RACKS. Wait 1/2 hour or more before slicing.

\+ + + + + + + + + + + + + + +

+ OVERNIGHT SURVIVAL BREAD +

Mix dough in the evening using only 1 package of yeast. In the morning, proceed as for the 4-hour recipe. The second rising, in the loaf pans, will also take a little longer. Baking time is the same.

+ + + + + + + + + + + + + +

+ HERB BREAD +

Substitute 1 tablespoon onion (or garlic) salt for regular salt. Cut sugar to 2 tablespoons instead of 4. Add 1 1/2 tablespoons mixed herbs (like bottled salad herbs or "fines herbes") to dry flour mixture; mix through before adding liquid. Proceed as usual.

SURVIVAL! - Things that go Bump in the Night -

"From Ghoulies and Ghosties,
And long-leggety Beasties,
And Things that go Bump in the Night
Good Lord deliver us!"
(Old Scottish Prayer)

Ghoulies, ghosties, and beasties - that's about the opinion most people have of the "scary" foods they think they don't like (they've never had them) and won't talk or even THINK about - the things known in cooking as "innards."

Innards do NOT go bump in the night. The quote is used here to make you remember this section of SURVIVAL! because innards are the greatest for survival, for taste, nutrition, and economy.

Stone Age Man knew what was good. He grew brawny and brainy and developed straight into the Bronze Age by chewing on parts we give to the cat. The frugal French, those clever Chinese, and all powerfully built peasant folk the world over delightedly chomp innards like we chew Chiclets.

It was only 20 years or so ago that nutritionists salvaged that most precious of parts, liver, from a trash-can fate and taught Americans its valuable properties. At the turn of the century, liver was given away free at the slaughterhouse. Now it's as much as $2.50 per pound.

But WHO will speak up for the rest of the innards? The heart, kidney, gizzards, wherein repose such a wealth of vitamins, minerals, and protein? You will!

They're still so cheap, can be prepared with such delectable results. Kick the habit of avoiding them. Discover innards before everyone else does and they all get to be $2.50 a pound.

+ + + + + + + + + + + + + +

+ PAWNBROKER'S STEW +

Preparation: 5 minutes
Cooking: 1 1/2 hours

Serves 2. A promise: It's perfectly delicious! But what is it? Well, remember giblet gravy? These are chicken giblets, baked to a tasty tenderness in cream sauce.

LINE UP YOUR INGREDIENTS:

1 1/2 lb. chicken giblets (gizzards)
1 can cream of chicken soup
2 teaspoons basil

Preheat oven to 400.

Wash giblets in cold water a minute. Dry them. Cut each into 6 or 8 small pieces with knife. Leave on yellow fat.

Grease pyrex casserole. Add cut up giblets. Sprinkle in basil. Pour in cream of chicken soup. Stir around well.

Cover. Bake on center rack of oven for 1 1/2 hours. Serve on rice (page 56) or buttered toast.

+ + + + + + + + + + + + + +

+ GAMBLER'S DICE +

Preparation: 15 minutes
Cooking: 1 1/2-2 hours

Serves 2. Here again our new found friends the giblets, this time cut up small and rechristened. Simple and cheap. If you're in a betting mood when you serve this, you can gamble on no one guessing what it is.

LINE UP YOUR INGREDIENTS:

1 1/2 lb. chicken giblets (gizzards)
2 strips bacon
1 large onion
2 tablespoons butter or margarine
1 1/2 teaspoons oregano
1 cup chicken broth (1 chicken bouillon cube dissolved in 1 cup hot water)
1 tablespoon flour
Some water

Separate giblets at connecting membranes. Cut into dice-size pieces. Cut bacon into dice-size pieces. Chop up peeled onion.

In large (12") skillet, melt better over medium heat. Add diced giblets. Brown 5-7 minutes, stirring now and then. Add chopped bacon, onion, and oregano. Stir, and cook 5 minutes.

Add chicken broth. Cover skillet. Turn heat to low. Simmer 1 1/4 hours.

In a small glass or cup, add just enough water to the flour to make a thick paste. Stir against sides with spoon till smooth. Add to giblet stew. Stir well. Cover. Simmer 15 minutes more. Serve on buttered toast.

+ + + + + + + + + + + + + +

+ PHILADELPHIA CREAMED KIDNEYS +

Preparation: 10 minutes
Cooking: 20 minutes

Serves 2. From the city of Brotherly Love comes this University of Pennsylvania lover-ly recipe. Please try it. It takes little money, little cooking time, and only a little nerve.

LINE UP YOUR INGREDIENTS:

6-8 small lamb kidneys
1 medium onion
Some water
1 tablespoon flour
1 can cream of mushroom soup
3 tablespoons butter or margarine

Split each kidney in half. With kitchen scissors or sharp knife, remove white fat. Remove thin membrane casings. Cut halves into 3 pieces each. Chop up peeled onion.

Put kidneys in saucepan. Add chopped onion. Pour in 1 cup water. Bring to a boil over high heat. Turn down to low. Cover pan. Simmer for 15 minutes.

Meanwhile: In a small glass or cup, add enough water to flour to make a smooth thick paste (1 or 2 tablespoons water). Stir well.

Pour flour-water paste into saucepan. Stir. Add can of cream of mushroom soup. Drop in 3 tablespoons butter.

Cover pan. Simmer 5-8 minutes. Serve on toast, rice, or thin noodles.

+ CHATTER +

If you choose to serve rice, remember to start cooking it way back when you start cooking the kidneys, as rice takes 20 minutes. Noodles, on the other hand take about 8-10 minutes.

+ + + + + + + + + + + + + +

+ STONED KIDNEYS +

Preparation: 10 minutes
Cooking time: 15 minutes

Serves 2. This recipe begs for Madeira wine. If that's breaking the budget, a California sherry will substitute. No matter which, the result is rich and heady.

LINE UP YOUR INGREDIENTS:

6-8 small lamb kidneys
1 medium onion
6 medium mushrooms
2 tablespoons butter or margarine
2 teaspoons flour
3/4 cup Madeira or sherry wine
1/2 teaspoon salt

Split kidneys in half. With kitchen scissors or sharp knife, remove white fat from each half. Also, remove thin membrane casing. Cut halves into 2 pieces.

Peel and chop onion. Cut mushroom caps in half. Cut mushroom stems in pieces.

Melt butter in large (12") skillet over medium-high heat. Add kidneys, onions, and mushrooms. Cook, stirring now and then, 4-5 minutes.

When kidneys are no longer pink, sprinkle flour over all. Stir well over heat for 1 minute to incorporate flour. Pour in wine. Add salt.

Bring to boil over high heat. Turn heat to low. Cover. Simmer 10 minutes. Serve on rice or noodles or toast.

+ + + + + + + + + + + + + +

+ THE LIVING-END BRAISED OXTAILS +

Preparation: 15 minutes
Cooking: 4 hours

Serves 2. Don't let the long cooking time turn you off this one. In the middle of winter nothing smells better in anticipation than this slow-cooker, and for a filling, peasanty stew, it's hard to beat. You don't need to add the "optional" ingredients, but if you want to make a meal-in-one-pot dish, the recipe says how.

LINE UP YOUR INGREDIENTS:

3-4 lb. oxtails
2 tablespoons flour
1 tablespoon salt
1 teaspoon pepper
2-3 tablespoons butter or margarine
1 teaspoon garlic powder
1 can Campbell's consomme
2-3 carrots (optional)
4 stalks celery (optional)
2 potatoes (optional)

Scrape oxtails with sharp knife. Cut off most fat. In small paper bag put flour, salt, and pepper. Shake each oxtail in bag with mixture till well coated.

Melt butter in large (12") skillet. Add oxtails. Brown 5 minutes on each side.

Sprinkle in garlic powder. Pour in consomme. Bring to boil over high heat. Cover. Turn down to low. Simmer for 4 hours.

If you are adding the vegetables: 45 minutes before oxtails are done, wash carrots, trim off ends, cut in 1" chunks, and add to pot. Also, cut up celery in 1" lengths, and add to pot. Peel potatoes. Cut in half. Add to pot.

Cover. Cook for remaining time, or till potatoes are fork tender.

+ LIVE-IT-UP CHICKEN LIVERS +

Preparation: 5 minutes
Cooking: 10 minutes

Serves 2. Everyone "knows" 3 facts about liver: They hate it; it looks terrible; it tastes like liver. But wait! Three more facts: It's one of the best dollar values; it is THE top meat nutritionally; it can, easily, be absolutely delicious. Take a chance. Live it up.

LINE UP YOUR INGREDIENTS:

2 slices bacon
1 large onion
1 lb. chicken livers
Salt and pepper
Toast (optional)
Eggs (optional)

Fry bacon in large (12") skillet till crisp. Remove to paper to drain.

Peel and chop onion. Add to bacon fat in skillet. Cook 3 to 4 minutes or until limp but not browned. With slotted spoon, remove onions to a side dish.

Dump chicken livers into fat in skillet. Cook over medium heat, stirring a bit and turning, till pink disappears (5 minutes).

Return onions to skillet with livers. Crumble bacon into skillet. Cover. Cook over low heat 10 minutes.

Serve, with pan juices, on buttered toast. Season to taste. OR, while livers are covered and simmering, scramble eggs in a separate skillet, and serve with the livers.

+ + + + + + + + + + + + + + +

+ WHAT'S-THE-BIG-BEEF LIVER +

Preparation: 2 minutes
Cooking: 10 minutes

Serves 2. Here's hoping the title will cheer you up and help you remember liver is, nutritionally, THE MOST OUTSTANDING meat you can buy. If that doesn't tempt you, the brief cooking time should.

LINE UP YOUR INGREDIENTS:

1 lb. baby-beef or lamb liver, sliced thin (1/4")
1/2 cup wheat germ
4 slices bacon
Salt
Pepper

Fry the bacon in large (12") skillet till crisp. Remove to paper to drain. Pour off all but about 2 tablespoons of bacon fat. Put skillet aside.

Pour wheat germ on counter top. Dredge (dip) both sides of liver in it.

Return skillet to stove. Heat bacon fat on medium-high heat. Put liver slices in skillet. Fry quickly, about 2 minutes each side.

Serve liver with slices of bacon on top. Season to taste. This, plus a green salad and baked potatoes (page 31), makes a great meal.

+ CHATTER +

Lacking wheat germ (tho' it's hoped you always stock it in your refrigerator), dredge the liver in flour.

+ + + + + + + + + + + + + +

+ HIGH-LIVING LIVER +

Preparation: 10 minutes
Cooking: 20 minutes

Serves 2. If you suspect this meat is being pushed in this chapter, you're right. The theory is, no one can be overexposed to liver. This recipe contains other seductions, so why resist?

LINE UP YOUR INGREDIENTS:

1 lb. baby beef or lamb liver, sliced 1/2" thick
Wheat germ or flour
4 slices bacon
3 medium onions
1 large green pepper
1/2 teaspoon thyme
1/2 teaspoon basil
1 teaspoon salt
1/4 cup dry red wine (Burgundy)

Preheat oven to 350. Grease a small casserole or bread-loaf pan.

Cut bacon in 1" pieces. Fry in large (12") skillet gently 3-4 minutes. Don't let it brown. Remove to paper to drain.

Dredge (dip) both sides of liver slices in wheat germ or flour (wheat germ tastes, and is, best). Quickly brown liver in skillet, 1-2 minutes each side at most. Remove from skillet.

Peel and slice onions thin. Chop up. Remove seeds from green pepper. Chop up pepper. Also crumble bacon.

Place liver, crumbled bacon, raw onions, and pepper in layers in greased casserole.

Into bowl or cup, measure thyme, basil, salt, and wine. Stir. Pour the seasoned wine over liver in casserole. Cover.

Place casserole on center rack in oven. Bake 20 minutes. This is good served with rice or boiled potatoes.

+ CHATTER +

Note that calf's liver has not been mentioned. It's too expensive, though delicious. As for pork liver, its cooking time is tricky and, for beginners, the flavor isn't all that reputable.

+ + + + + + + + + + + + + +

Useful MISCELLANY Department

Most measurements (like a cup or teaspoon) should be level. Level off dry ingredients with the back of a knife.

A "cup" is definite measurement, not just any old coffee cup or bra size. You can buy measuring cups in 1-cup and 2-cup sizes.

Note that there are always 3 teaspoons in 1 tablespoon. Nobody knows why. Any old spoons won't really do. Buy measuring spoons.

When measuring things in quantity, count out loud.

Don't try to measure out something precise, like a cake, while idly chatting. You'll probably leave out or miscount some key ingredient.

Cooking temperatures should not be altered in this or any other cookbook. If something is to be cooked 2 hours at 250 (oven temperature), you shouldn't try 1 hour at 500 or you'll have burned outside, raw insides, etc. Centuries of experimentation has decreed the best cooking temperatures for specific meats and cuts to produce tenderness.

Broiling hamburgers dries them out. Put a chip of ice inside each burger to keep center moist and juicy.

If frying steak, baloney, ham, sliced sausage, etc., make several small cuts in edges to prevent meat curling up.

Keep noodles, spaghetti from boiling over by adding 1 teaspoon cooking oil to water. Or leave a long-handled wooden spoon standing in the pot.

Tests for spaghetti doneness: Usually cook it 8 minutes. Taste it. Or, throw a strand of spaghetti on the wall or against the refrigerator. If it sticks, it's done. If it slithers to the floor, it's not done. Which will be your spaghetti wall?

+ + + + + + + + + + + + + +

All vegetables should be refrigerated until just before cooking. Light and warmth break down vitamin content.

Fresh parsley stays fresh much longer if washed and stored in tightly covered jar in the refrigerator.

Keep cans of olives, pickles, bacon grease, jam, etc., that have been opened in the refrigerator.

Refrigerate flour that contains wheat germ (like stone-ground flour) to prevent invasion of weevils (little beetles).

Refrigerate all cheese. For best flavor, remove to room temperature a few hours before eating - it makes a big difference.

If mold develops on cheese, cut it off with a knife dipped in vinegar. To keep cheese longer without mold, wrap in a cloth (cheese cloth?) dipped in vinegar.

When refrigerating uncooked meats, remove from store package to plate, cover loosely with paper or plastic.

Most uncooked meats will refrigerate safely up to 5 days. Exceptions are hamburger, which should be cooked within 3 days. Kidneys, liver, and fresh fish should be cooked within 2 days of purchase. After cooking, meats may be refrigerated safely again for several days.

About spoiled meats: Before the days of refrigeration, slightly spoiled meats were common. Cooks washed them with water and baking soda to remove the bad smell, then prepared them with spicy herbs to remove any further trace of odor. This accounts for the highly spiced foods common to tropical countries (the curries of India, the peppery foods of Mexico) and explains Columbus's search for new spice routes. But for you, when in doubt about meat spoilage (you'll know, there's that odor!), throw it out.

About freezing: You can freeze raw meats, then cook and freeze them again. But you must <u>not</u> freeze cooked meats a <u>second</u> time because of dangerous bacteria which may have multiplied during the thaw. You could get quite sick.

If your refrigerator has a separate freezer inside main door, keep freezer door tight shut to prevent frost buildup.

To defrost freezer quickly, borrow a girl's hair dryer, direct hot air inside. To prevent ice from re-forming so quickly in freezer (and to make defrosting easier), rub inside with cooking oil.

If refrigerator develops odd odor, find out what's doing it (cover it or throw it out), then place a few chunks of charcoal inside. Or wash refrigerator with water and baking soda or a damp towel with a drop or two of vanilla.

+ + + + + + + + + + + + + +

Don't throw away old bread. Use it for French Toast or Croutons.

Refresh dried-out bread and rolls by reheating in a paper bag which has been sprinkled with water. Heat in 400 oven for 10 minutes.

One average tea bag will make 4 cups of tea if mixed with boiling water, in a pot, and allowed to steep.

If making instant coffee in quantity, use 3 teaspoons (or less, depending upon brand) to make 4 cups of coffee.

If honey crystallizes, set the jar in a pan of very hot water.

In cool weather, keep some butter at room temperature in a small dish or old cheese crock. You use less and it's easier to spread.

A few grains of uncooked rice added to salt shakers will absorb humidity, let salt pour easier.

Lemons and oranges yield quite a bit more juice if dropped briefly into hot water before squeezing.

If heating milk, rub a little butter in pan bottom to prevent milk from sticking. Makes clean-up easier.

To tell a hard-boiled egg from a raw egg, spin them. The hard-boiled egg spins nicely, the raw egg wobbles.

To open fresh coconuts: Islanders use a special method to prevent meat from sticking to the shell. With a heavy knife handle, or hammer, tap the 3 soft spots on the top. Pierce one, pour off milk. (Drink it, or add it to any other juice.)

Now, revolve the nut with one hand while you gently tap the entire surface of the shell with the hammer. Keep this up, restraining yourself from bashing it, and the entire shell will fall off. With a sharp knife, slice off the brown-paper skin from the meat.

This does take a few minutes but is much easier than trying to pick meat out of a broken shell.

+ + + + + + + + + + + + + +

When shopping, you don't have to purchase 6 of something (like green peppers or lemons) because they're packaged that way. Ask for less or more. Clerks are there to serve. Right?

Canned foods, by law, list all ingredients and whatever is listed first is in the greatest proportion. (Note how many expensive cans of corned-beef hash list potatoes first, because they contain more potatoes than beef.)

A small cheap blackboard in the kitchen is handy to note shopping needs. People don't seem to steal chalk.

If you're not keen on aprons, tuck a cloth kitchen towel in your belt.

Wipe greasy stove tops, etc., first with a paper towel, then go over with a wet sponge. It's easier.

Scour wooden cutting board with baking soda, not scouring powder. Keeps soap out of foods.

Douse a cooking fire (like burning grease) quickly with ordinary table salt. Use a lot.

If you burn yourself, flood burn with cold water. If it's at all bad, hold a plastic bag of ice cubes on burn for 30 minutes or more. Solarcaine is good to have in the kitchen, not the bathroom.

Alcoholic beverages can cause brain damage because they remove B vitamins from the brain. In case you intend to get drunk, counteract the effect by loading up with vitamin-B complex. If you want to remain an observer a little longer at the party, drink a big glass of milk before imbibing. Coats the insides.

Chew fresh parsley to get rid of garlic odor on breath.

Many dentists recommend the occasional use of baking soda for really shiny, clean teeth.

Get rid of onion or garlic odor on hands by rubbing them with vinegar, or a slice of lemon, or mouthwash, or rubbing wet hands with salt.

Cut raw onions left open to air change their chemistry, become almost inedible. But, try a raw onion to absorb fresh-paint smells.

Kitty litter will clean up car oil (and dog) spills. Remove stains (dog and other) from rug with club soda or 1 tablespoon of white vinegar in a cup of water.

Candles will last longer and drip less if you put them into the refrigerator for a few hours before using.

A good high-protein shampoo is 1 egg yolk mixed with 1 cup warm - not hot - water. Rub all through hair, massaging till scalp tingles (2-3 minutes). Rinse with warm - not hot - water, else you'll end up with scrambled hair.

If you object to the taste of glue on postage stamps, lick the corner of the envelope where the stamp goes, press the stamp on the wet spot.

\+ + + + + + + + + + + + + +

RECIPE INDEX